Cell
714-404-624

Airline Transport Pilot
Oral Exam Guide

by Michael D. Hayes

Second Edition

The comprehensive
guide to prepare you
for the FAA checkride

Aviation Supplies & Academics, Inc.
Newcastle, Washington

Airline Transport Pilot Oral Exam Guide
Second Edition
by Michael D. Hayes

Aviation Supplies & Academics, Inc.
7005 132nd Place SE
Newcastle, Washington 98059-3153

Visit the ASA website often (**www.asa2fly.com**, Product Updates link or search "OEG-ATP") to find updates posted there due to FAA regulation revisions that may affect this book. See also **www.asa2fly.com/reader/oegatp** for the "Reader Resources" page with extra source material to download.

Printed in the United States of America

2014   2013   2012   2011   9   8   7   6   5   4   3   2   1

ASA-OEG-ATP2
ISBN 1-56027-863-3
      978-1-56027-863-4

Library of Congress Cataloging-in-Publication Data:

Hayes, Michael D.
    Airline transport pilot oral exam guide: the comprehensive
    guide to prepare you for the FAA Oral exam / by Michael D.
    Hayes.
            p.   cm.
    Includes bibliographical references.
    1. Airplanes—Piloting—Examinations—Study guides.
    2. Airplanes—Piloting—Examinations, questions, etc.
    3. Air pilots—Licenses—United States. I. Title.
TL710.H36 2001
629.132'5216'076—dc21   2001053275

This guide is dedicated to the many talented students, pilots and flight instructors I have had the opportunity to work with over the years. Also, special thanks to Mark Hayes and many others who supplied the patience, encouragement, and understanding necessary to complete the project.

—M.D.H.

Contents

Introduction

The *ATP Oral Exam Guide* is a comprehensive guide designed for pilots who are involved in training for the Airline Transport Pilot Certificate. The ATP OEG will also prove beneficial for those pilots transitioning to turbine aircraft or who have been accepted and are preparing for entry into an initial training course at an airline ground school.

The Airline Transport Pilot Practical Test Standards book (FAA-H-8081-5) specifies the subject areas in which knowledge must be demonstrated by the applicant before issuance of an Airline Transport Pilot certificate with the associated category and class ratings. The *ATP Oral Exam Guide* contains questions pertaining to those areas as well as other areas of operations critical to flight safety, such as aeronautical decision making, crew resource management, and wake turbulence avoidance.

Questions and answers are organized into six chapters. The first two chapters cover basic turbine aircraft theory, performance and limitations. The next four chapters include information on airline operational procedures, aeronautical decision-making and crew resource management, regulations (Parts 61, 121, and 135), and instrument procedures.

At the end of this guide are two appendices that contain questions and answers that might be asked in a typical airline-type ride, concerning aircraft systems and limitations. All questions and answers reference information specific to a Beechcraft 1900C aircraft. Although systems will vary from aircraft to aircraft, this particular aircraft is representative of a typical turboprop aircraft found in many of today's regional airline aircraft fleets and is used so the pilot can learn the basic components and principles, which remain the same. None of the material in the *ATP Oral Exam Guide* supersedes any aircraft manual, procedure, or document published for the Beechcraft 1900C aircraft.

Continued

The *ATP Oral Exam Guide* may be supplemented with other comprehensive study materials as noted in parentheses after each question, for example (AC 65-12). The abbreviations for these materials and their titles are listed below. If no reference is given after a question, the answer for that question was researched from interviews with airline pilots, 121/135 operators, and examiners. Be sure to use the latest references when reviewing for the test. Also, check the ASA website at www.asa2fly.com for the latest updates to this book on our "Product Updates" page; all the latest changes in FAA procedures and regulations that affect these questions will be listed there.

14 CFR Part 1	*Definitions and Abbreviations*
14 CFR Part 61	*Certification: Pilots, Flight Instructors, and Ground Instructors*
14 CFR Part 91	*General Operating and Flight Rules*
14 CFR Part 117	(New rule pending) *Flight and Duty Limitations and Rest Requirements for all Flightcrew Members and Certificate Holders*
14 CFR Part 119	*Certification: Air Carriers and Commercial Operators*
14 CFR Part 121	*Operating Requirements: Domestic, Flag, and Supplemental Operations*
14 CFR Part 125	*Certification and Operations: Airplanes Having a Seating Capacity of 20 or More Passengers or a Maximum Payload Capacity of 6,000 Pounds or More; and Rules Governing Persons on Board Such Aircraft*
14 CFR Part 135	*Operating Requirements: Commuter and On-Demand Operations and Rules Governing Persons On Board Such Aircraft*
AC 00-6	*Aviation Weather*
AC 00-33	*Nickel-Cadmium Battery Operational, Maintenance and Overhaul Practices*
AC 00-45	*Aviation Weather Services*
AC 00-54	*Pilot Windshear Guide*
AC 60-22	*Aeronautical Decision Making*
AC 61-84	*Role of Preflight Preparation*
AC 61-107	*Operations of Aircraft at Altitudes Above 25,000 Feet MSL and/or Mach Number Greater Than 0.75*
AC 61-134	*General Aviation Controlled Flight into Terrain Awareness*

AC 65-12	*A&P Mechanics Powerplant Handbook*
AC 65-15	*A&P Mechanics Airframe Handbook*
AC 90-94	*Guidelines for Using GPS Equipment for IFR En Route and Terminal Operations*
AC 91-51	*Effects of Icing on Aircraft Control and Airplane Deice and Anti-ice Systems*
AC 91-74	*Pilot Guide: Flight in Icing Conditions*
AC 120-12	*Private Carriage Versus Common Carriage of Persons or Property*
AC 120-27	*Aircraft Weight and Balance Control*
AC 120-28	*Criteria for Approval of CAT III Landing Weather Minima for Takeoff, Landing, and Rollout*
AC 120-29	*Criteria for Approval of CAT I and II Weather Minima for Approach*
AC 120-51	*Crew Resource Management Training*
AC 120-60	*Ground Deicing and Anti-icing Program*
AC 120-62	*Takeoff Safety Training Aid*
AC 120-71	*Standard Operating Procedures for Flight Deck Crewmembers*
AFM	*Airplane Flight Manual*
AIM	*Aeronautical Information Manual*
P/CG	This is the *Pilot/Controller Glossary* included in the AIM.
Order 8900.1	*Flight Standards Information Management System (FSIMS)*
JO 7210.754	*Line Up and Wait (LUAW) Operations*
FAA-H-8081-5	*Airline Transport Pilot Practical Test Standards*
FAA-H-8083-1	*Aircraft Weight and Balance Handbook*
FAA-H-8083-2	*Risk Management Handbook*
FAA-H-8083-3	*Airplane Flying Handbook*
FAA-H-8083-6	*Advanced Avionics Handbook*
FAA-H-8083-9	*Aviation Instructor's Handbook*
FAA-H-8083-15	*Instrument Flying Handbook*
FAA-H-8083-25	*Pilot's Handbook of Aeronautical Knowledge*
FAA-H-8083-30	*Aviation Maintenance Technician Handbook—General*
FAA-H-8261-1	*Instrument Procedures Handbook*
FAA-P-8740-19	*Flying Light Twins Safely*

Turbine
Aircraft Systems

1

A. Engine

1. How does a gas turbine engine work? (AC 65-12A)

A gas turbine engine is designed to extract energy from a stream of hot, high velocity gases that have been accelerated through use of the following three basic components:

a. A compressor—compresses incoming air to high pressure.

b. A combustion chamber—ignites and burns fuel to produce high pressure/high velocity gases.

c. A turbine—extracts energy from the high pressure/high velocity gases exiting the combustion chamber.

The single greatest factor influencing the construction features of any gas turbine engine is the type of compressor (axial flow or centrifugal flow) for which the engine is designed.

2. Describe a centrifugal-flow compressor. (AC 65-12A)

This compressor has an impeller surrounded by a ring of diffuser vanes. The impeller is driven at high speed by a turbine. Air is drawn into the air inlet and directed to the center of the impeller. The air is then forced outward centrifugally into a diffuser, where the pressure of the air is increased. The pressurized air is then supplied to the combustion section.

3. Describe an axial-flow compressor. (AC 65-12A)

This consists of two main elements, a rotor and a stator. The rotor, turning at high speeds, has blades fixed on a spindle that takes in air at the compressor inlet and impels it rearward through a series of stages paralleling the longitudinal axis of the engine. The action of the rotor increases the compression of the air at each stage, accelerating it rearward through several stages. With this increased velocity, energy is transferred from the compressor to the air in the form of velocity energy. The stator blades act as diffusers at each stage, partially converting high velocity to pressure. Each consecutive pair of rotor and stator blades constitutes a pressure stage; the greater the number of stages, the higher the compression ratio. Most present-day engines utilize from 10 to 16 stages.

4. What are the main types of gas turbine engines?
(AC 65-12A)

a. *Turbojet*—is the most fundamental gas turbine engine. The relatively small frontal area results in a small mass of air accelerated through the core to a high velocity; no fan is utilized. Air is compressed, ignited in the combustion section, and expelled at the rear of the engine at high velocity to drive a turbine, which in turn drives a compressor. Used on aircraft that fly at high airspeeds and altitudes. Inefficient and loud at low altitudes.

b. *Turbofan*—a gas turbine engine with a duct-enclosed axial flow fan at the front of the engine, driven by the engine's turbine section. A portion of the incoming air entering the engine is compressed and enters a combustion chamber; the other portion is also compressed and bypasses the combustion section altogether. Both are joined together downstream to produce thrust. In high bypass engines, the fan/bypass air produces most of the thrust. The two types of turbofan engines, low bypass and high bypass, refers to the amount of air bypassing the core. Turbofan engines are a compromise between turbojet and turboprop engines, resulting in better high-altitude performance than the turboprop, and better low-altitude performance than the turbojet.

c. *Turboprop*—basically a turbojet engine that utilizes exhaust gases to turn a propeller. Two methods are used: 1) high-velocity exhaust gases turn a propeller directly via a compressor shaft and reduction gear box; or 2) exhaust gases turn a power turbine, which is connected to the propeller via a shaft and reduction gear box. A turboprop engine moves a large mass of air at a low velocity and is the ideal application for low-altitude and lower speed aircraft.

d. *Turboshaft*—much like a turboprop engine; high velocity exhaust gases turn a power turbine connected to a rotor via a shaft and reduction gearbox. Normally used in helicopters where a turboshaft turns both the main and tail rotors.

5. What are the basic components of a turboprop engine? (AC 65-12A)

The typical turboprop engine can be broken down into assemblies as follows:

a. The power section assembly with the major components of gas turbine engines (compressor, combustion chamber, turbine, and exhaust sections);

b. The reduction gear or gearbox assembly—those sections peculiar to turboprop configurations;

c. The torquemeter assembly, which transmits the torque from the engine to the gearbox of the reduction section; and

d. The accessory drive housing assembly.

6. What does N1 and N2 indicate? (FAA-H-8083-3)

N1 is the rotational speed of the gas generator's low-pressure compressor/turbine in a dual compressor engine. *N2* is the rotational speed of the gas generator's high-pressure compressor/turbine in a dual compressor engine.

7. Define the term "ITT." (FAA-H-8083-3)

Interstage Turbine Temperature (ITT)—the temperature of the gases between the high pressure and low pressure turbine wheels.

8. What is the definition of a "hot start" and a "hung start"? (FAA-H-8083-3)

Hot start—this is when normal engine rotation occurs, but with exhaust temperature exceeding prescribed limits; usually caused by an excessively rich mixture in the combustor. Fuel to the engine must be terminated immediately to prevent engine damage.

Hung start—a condition in which normal "light-off" occurs yet engine RPM remains at a low value rather than increasing to the normal idle speed; often the result of insufficient power to the engine from the starter. The engine should be shut down immediately.

9. What are igniters? (AC 65-12A)

The typical gas turbine engine is equipped with "igniters" that provide a high heat intensity spark used to ignite the fuel-air mixture. A typical ignition system includes two exciter units, two transformers, two intermediate ignition leads, and two high-tension leads. As a safety factor, the ignition system is actually a dual system, designed to fire two igniter plugs. This type of ignition system provides a high degree of reliability under widely varying conditions of altitude, atmospheric pressure, temperature, fuel vaporization, and input voltage.

10. What are thrust reversers? (AC 65-12A)

In turboprop aircraft, the reversible pitch propeller acts as a thrust reverser by re-directing thrust forward. In turbojet/turbofan engines, a thrust reverser is a device installed in the exhaust gas stream, usually somewhat to the rear of the nozzle. The engine exhaust gases are mechanically blocked and diverted in the reverse direction by an inverted cone, half sphere, or other means of obstruction, which is placed in position to reverse the flow of exhaust gases. They significantly reduce landing distances, as well as brake fade, and contribute to extended tire life. There are two types, mechanical blockage and aerodynamic, and they are sometimes referred to as clamshell, cascade, or petal-door type thrust reversers.

11. What are the two basic types of turbine engine lubrication systems? (AC 65-12A)

Both wet- and dry-sump lubrication systems are used in gas turbine engines. Most turbojet engines are of the axial-flow configuration, and use a dry-sump lubrication system. However, some turbine engines are equipped with a combination dry and wet type of lubrication system.

12. What is the main difference between wet- and dry-sump lubrication systems? (AC 65-12A)

Wet-sump engines store the lubricating oil in the engine proper, while dry-sump engines use an external tank that is usually mounted on the engine (or somewhere in the aircraft structure near the engine).

13. How is the oil cooled in a turbine engine? (AC 65-12A)

To ensure proper temperature, oil is routed through either an air-cooled or a fuel-cooled oil cooler. With an oil-to-fuel heat exchanger, not only is heat removed from the oil but the fuel is kept at proper temperature, thus eliminating the potential for ice formation within the fuel.

B. Propeller

1. What is a propeller governor? (AC 65-12A)

This "governs" propeller RPM by sensing changes in it and hydraulically changing the propeller pitch to compensate for the change in RPM. Turboprop aircraft use three types of governors to accomplish this:

a. Primary governor—controls oil pressure supplied to propeller hub.

b. Overspeed governor—has the additional task of protecting against propeller overspeed condition by automatically draining supply pressure.

c. Fuel-topping governor—provides secondary protection against an overspeed condition by restricting fuel flow to the engine.

2. What is beta range? (FAA-H-8083-3)

The non-governing or taxi range aft of the "idle" stop and forward of the "reverse" position is referred to as the "beta" range. In beta range, the power levers control only prop pitch and torque remains constant. In this range, a "beta valve" commands the lowest possible propeller pitch for a specific power lever position. Beta range permits prop pitch to be reduced to zero-thrust settings for slowing and taxiing without a change to gas generator RPM.

3. Describe a typical autofeather system. (AC 65-12A)

An autofeather system automatically feathers a propeller when engine power loss results in a propeller thrust drop to a preset value. This system is switch-armed for use during takeoff and can function only when the power lever is near or in the "takeoff" position. When an autofeather system senses an engine failure, it will automatically begin dumping oil from the propeller servo of the failed engine to enable the propeller to go into a feathered condition with assistance from feathering springs and counterweights. A very important feature on turboprop aircraft, considering the size of the propellers and the amount of drag they produce in the event of an engine failure.

4. Explain how a propeller synchrophaser/synchronizer system functions. (FAA-H-8083-3)

A propeller synchrophaser/synchronizer automatically equalizes rotational speeds of both propellers by comparing the control engine's propeller RPM/phase angle to the slave engine's RPM/ phase angle, electronically adjusting the prop governor of one engine to the other in order to keep the propeller RPM and/or blade phase angle relationship the same. Greatly reduces the noise level and vibration within the airplane and eliminates the unpleasant beat produced by unsynchronized propeller operation.

5. What is a reduction gearbox? (AC 65-12A)

The increased brake horsepower output of gas turbine engines requires reduction gearing to limit the propeller rotation speed (relative to the speed of the power turbine) to a value at which efficient operation is obtained. Whenever the speed of the blade tips approaches the speed of sound, the efficiency of the propeller decreases rapidly.

C. Electrical

1. Describe some of the advantages and disadvantages of NiCad batteries. (FAA-H-8083-30)

Nickel-cadmium batteries are used frequently in turboprop aircraft. They have both some advantages and disadvantages:

Advantages:

a. Long service life and excellent reliability.

b. Can maintain sustained voltage until almost completely discharged.

c. Deliver large amounts of current.

d. Short recharge time after heavy use.

Disadvantages:

a. Relatively expensive.

b. Temperature sensitive.

c. Thermal runaway problem.

d. Battery memory can prevent battery from fully recharging.

2. What is thermal runaway? (AC 00-33A)

Basically, "thermal runaway" is an uncontrollable rise in battery temperature that will ultimately destroy the battery. This condition can occur when a nickel-cadmium battery is operated at above normal temperatures and is subjected to high charging currents associated with constant voltage charging. As the temperature of the battery increases, the effective internal resistance decreases and higher current is drawn from the constant voltage charging source. The higher current increases the battery temperature, which in turn results in even higher charging currents and temperatures.

3. Describe lead-acid batteries. (FAA-H-8083-30)

A common type of battery used in small aircraft as well as some turbine aircraft. The cells of the battery are connected in series. In discharging, the chemical energy stored in the battery is changed to electrical energy; in charging, the electrical energy supplied to the battery is changed to chemical energy and stored. Each cell of a lead acid battery normally develops 2 volts. The most common lead acid batteries are 12 or 24 volt and are rated in amp hours. An amp-hour equals 1 amp delivered for 1 hour.

4. What is a generator? (FAA-H-8083-30)

Any device that converts mechanical energy into electrical energy by electromagnetic induction. AC and DC generators are the most common types; both operate by inducing an AC voltage in coils varying the amount and direction of the magnetic flux cutting through the coils.

5. Describe the function of a starter-generator unit.
(AC 65-12A)

Many gas turbine aircraft are equipped with starter-generator systems that use a combination starter-generator, which operates as a starter motor to drive the engine during starting, then operates as a generator to supply the electrical system power after the engine has reached a self-sustaining speed.

6. Describe generator control units (GCUs).
(FAA-H-8083-30)

GCUs are multifunction electrical components that provide electrical system control and protective functions such as:

a. Voltage regulation

b. Over-voltage protection

c. Load paralleling between generators

d. Automatic cancellation of start cycle

e. Reverse polarity protection

7. What are inverters? (FAA-H-8083-30)

Inverters are used in some aircraft systems to convert a portion of the aircraft's DC power to AC power, which is used mainly for instruments, radio, radar, lighting, and other accessories. There are two types of inverters, rotary and static; they are usually designed to supply current at a frequency of 400 cps. Some are designed to provide more than one voltage; for example, 26 volt AC in one winding and 115 volts in another.

8. Why do most large aircraft use AC power rather than DC power? (FAA-H-8083-30)

Alternating current has largely replaced direct current in commercial power systems for a number of reasons:

a. It can be transmitted over long distances more readily and more economically than direct current, since AC voltages can be increased or decreased by means of transformers.

b. Space and weight can be saved, since AC devices, especially motors, are smaller and simpler than DC devices.

c. In most AC motors, no brushes are required so commutation trouble at high altitude is eliminated.

d. Circuit breakers operate satisfactorily under load at high altitudes in an AC system, whereas arcing is so excessive in DC systems that circuit breakers must be replaced frequently.

e. Most airplanes using a 24-volt DC system have special equipment that requires a certain amount of 400-cycle AC current, making it necessary to convert with inverters.

9. What is an electrical bus bar? (FAA-H-8083-3)

A common electrical system component that interfaces power from a common source, such as a generator, to a variety of electrical components connected to the bus. Most transport category aircraft use multiple bus systems, allowing for a certain degree of redundancy in the event of a failure of any one component.

10. What are electrical bus ties? (FAA-H-8083-3)

A bus tie is an electrical switch that connects (or disconnects) different electrical buses. Bus ties provide a means of isolating a powered bus from one that has failed. They can also redirect power to buses that have lost their primary power source.

11. What is a rectifier? (FAA-H-8083-30)

A rectifier is a device that transforms alternating current (AC) into direct current (DC) by limiting or regulating the direction of current flow. Rectifiers provide a simple and efficient method of obtaining high voltage DC at low amperage. They can also be an excellent source of high amperage at low voltage, depending on the type of rectifier used.

12. What is a diode? (FAA-H-8083-30)

A two-element electrical device that allows current to travel in one direction only. Sometimes thought of as an electronic check valve.

13. What is a hot battery bus? (FAA-H-8083-3)

An electrical bus that is directly connected to the battery. Usually contains items that might be needed in a complete electrical system failure, such as emergency lights, communication radio, engine fire extinguishing, etc.

14. What is a transformer? (FAA-H-8083-30)

A transformer changes electrical energy of a given voltage into electrical energy at a different voltage level.

15. What is a relay? (FAA-H-8083-30)

Relays, or relay switches, are electrical switches used for remote control of circuits carrying heavy currents. A relay is connected in the circuit between the unit controlled and the nearest source of power (or power bus bar) so that the cables carrying heavy current will be as short as possible. A relay consists of a coil or solenoid, an iron coil, and both fixed and movable contacts.

16. What is a solenoid? (FAA-H-8083-30)

An electromagnetically operated switch with a moveable core. Used to operate a variety of devices including switches, valves, and electromechanical devices.

17. What are several types of circuit protection devices? (FAA-H-8083-30)

a. *Circuit breaker*—designed to break the circuit and stop the current flow when the current exceeds a predetermined value.

b. *Fuse*—a strip of metal that will melt when current in excess of its carefully determined capacity flows through it. Installed in a circuit so that all the current in that circuit passes through it; usually made of an alloy of tin and bismuth.

c. *Current limiter*—a fuse made of copper used primarily to sectionalize an aircraft circuit.

18. **Define the following electrical system troubleshooting terms: short circuit, open circuit.** (FAA-H-8083-30)

A short circuit is a low-resistance path. It can be across the power source or between the sides of a circuit. It usually creates high current flow, which will burn out or cause damage to the circuit conductor or components.

An open circuit is one that is not complete or continuous.

D. Fuel

1. **What are the components of a typical fuel system?** (AC 65-12A)

a. *Fuel tanks*—wing and collector, surge vent, and drain collector tanks; often interconnected.

b. *Vent system*—fuel vents, sometimes heated, NACA air intake, vent valves, float vent valves, flame arrestors.

c. *Pumps*—high-pressure, low-pressure, electric boost, and jet pumps.

d. *Valves*—pressure relief, check, emergency shutoff, crossfeed shutoff, motive-flow shutoff, and fueling shutoff valves.

e. *Filters*—low- and high-pressure filters; usually include a bypass sensor and valve.

f. *Fuel heaters*—usually oil/fuel heat exchanger (uses heat from engine oil) or air/fuel heat exchanger (uses heat from engine bleed air).

g. *Fuel temperature sensors*—located in fuel line downstream from fuel heater.

h. *Fuel quantity measurement system*—capacitance fuel quantity indicator system, fuel quantity measuring sticks (allows manual measurement of fuel quantity).

i. *Fuel control units*—mechanical (hydromechanical) FCUs, FADECs (full authority digital engine controls), EECs (electronic engine controls), ECUs (electronic control units).

2. Describe the different types of fuel pumps found on turboprop aircraft. (AC 65-12A)

a. *High pressure pump* — usually engine-driven gear type pump; provides majority of fuel to engine.

b. *Low pressure pump* — usually engine-driven or motive-flow type jet pump; supplies main engine-driven pump with fuel.

c. *Electric boost pumps* — used for engine start, fuel crossfeed, main jet pump failure, pressure de-fuel.

d. *Jet pumps* — motive-flow type pumps; used to keep collector tanks at operational levels as well as provide constant fuel flow to the main pumps.

3. What is a fuel control unit? (AC 65-12A)

A fuel control unit is a device used on gas turbine engines to first determine and then meter the appropriate amount of fuel required by the engine for a given set of conditions. These conditions include such variables as power lever position, engine RPM, temperature and pressure. Fuel control units can be divided into two basic groups: (1) hydromechanical and (2) electronic. The electronic fuel control is a combination of the two basic groups. FADECs, EECs, and ECUs are examples of electronic fuel control units.

4. What are the two methods used to prevent ice crystals from forming in the fuel? (AC 65-12A)

a. An engine oil-to-fuel heat exchanger is located in the system prior to the engine driven fuel pump. Heat from the engine oil maintains the fuel at the correct temperature.

b. Fuel-air heat exchangers that use hot bleed air to maintain fuel at the correct temperature.

5. What is a collector tank?

A fuel tank within a fuel tank. It is an integral part of the inboard tank at the lowest point (closest to fuselage). The tank ensures a constant fuel level and continuous supply of fuel to the engine during normal maneuvering.

6. What is a jet pump?

A type of hydraulic pump that operates solely by motive flow. The jet pump utilizes the venturi effect to create a low-pressure area, which starts the motive-flow action and draws fuel into the lines. The venturi effect is established by passing high-velocity, engine-driven or electric-pump fuel through a venturi. Jet pumps are for a variety of purposes:

a. Provides a constant fuel flow to the main pumps.

b. Maintains collector tanks at operational levels.

c. Acts as secondary pumps for the main pumps.

d. Fuel vapor collectors from fuel tanks and fuel control units.

7. What is motive flow?

A flow created by the suction of a low-pressure area created by a venturi.

8. Describe the various types of fuel vents.

A NACA vent is an aerodynamically shaped vent installed on a wing to vent or equalize internal fuel tank pressure to the outside air; used due to the very low drag characteristic and resistance to structural icing. (NACA: National Advisory Committee for Aeronautics, which has since been replaced by NASA.)

A flame arrestor vent is a fuel vent with a wire-mesh screen that prevents accidental ignition of fuel vapors by lightning, hot exhaust, etc., from igniting fuel in the tanks.

A vent valve is a type of valve in the fuel tank of a wing that equalizes internal fuel tank pressure with the outside air pressure. Also prevents fuel tank overpressurization during fueling operations.

9. Describe the operation of fuel quantity measuring sticks.

Fuel quantity measuring sticks provide a pilot with a method to manually measure the fuel quantity in each wing tank. This system usually consists of several hollow tubes extended into the fuel cell from the bottom of each tank. Within each of these hollow tubes is a stick that can be unlocked and lowered until fuel begins dripping out of the stick, indicating the top of the stick is at or just below the fuel level in the tank.

More recent systems utilize magnetic "dripless" sticks. A magnet at the top of each stick, once unlocked, aligns itself with a magnetic float within the fuel tank, thus indicating the fuel level within the tank.

E. Hydraulic

1. A typical hydraulic system consists of what basic components? (AC 65-15A)

a. Main engine driven pumps

b. Electric hydraulic pumps

c. Hydraulic reservoirs

d. Valves — shutoff, check, drain

e. Various filters, sensors, switches and accumulators

2. What is a hydraulic accumulator? (AC 65-15A)

A device that stores hydraulic pressure, the basic components of which are a piston and a cylinder, with one side of the piston pressurized with nitrogen and the other side by hydraulic pressure. The nitrogen is compressed as hydraulic pressure is applied. When hydraulic pressure is required, a valve is opened allowing hydraulic fluid to flow. The hydraulic lines are pressurized as a result of the pressurized nitrogen forcing hydraulic fluid out of the accumulator.

3. What is a hydraulic actuator? (AC 65-15A)

A device that utilizes hydraulic pressure to move something mechanically. Sometimes used to extend and retract the gear and flaps.

4. What is pump cavitation?

This occurs when air in the hydraulic lines enters the hydraulic pump, causing the pump to be unable to move hydraulic fluid. The pump eventually overheats and fails since it depends on fluid movement for cooling. This condition can occur for several reasons, such as the hydraulic reservoir fluid level being too low, or foaming of the hydraulic fluid.

5. What are hydraulic fuses?

Hydraulic fuses are hydromechanical flow-control valves installed in aircraft hydraulic lines, which are designed to prevent excessive or complete loss of all hydraulic fluid in the event of a ruptured hydraulic line.

F. Landing Gear

1. What components are used in a typical hydraulic landing gear system? (AC 65-15)

These include engine-driven and electrical hydraulic pumps, actuating cylinders, selector valves, solenoids, uplocks, downlocks, sequence valves, emergency override controls, tubing, and other conventional hydraulic components.

2. Describe the operational sequence of a typical hydraulic landing gear system.

a. *Extension:*

  i. A selector lever in the cockpit electrically commands the gear to extend.

  ii. A solenoid valve directs hydraulic pressure to the extension side of system.

  iii. Sequencing valves hold the landing gear in place until the landing gear doors have opened.

  iv. With gear doors open, hydraulic pressure causes uplocks to be released and hydraulic pressure is applied to the actuators to extend the gear.

Continued

      v. Once extended, downlocks are positioned hydraulically.

     vi. Landing gear position switches provide indicating system with information on gear position.

    vii. Sequencing valves direct hydraulic pressure to close the landing gear doors.

  b. *Retraction:*

      i. A selector lever in the cockpit electrically commands the gear to retract.

     ii. Landing gear position switches provide indicating system with information on gear position (in-transit).

    iii. A solenoid valve directs hydraulic pressure to the retraction side of system.

    iv. Sequencing valves prevent the landing gear from retracting until the landing gear doors have opened.

     v. With gear doors now open, hydraulic pressure is applied to the actuators to retract the gear.

     vi. Wheel rotation is stopped by hydraulic pressure routed to the brake system.

    vii. Landing gear uplocks are positioned.

   viii. Landing gear position switches provide indicating system with information on gear position (up and locked).

     ix. Sequencing valves direct hydraulic pressure to close the landing gear doors.

3. How does a landing gear "safety" switch function?
(AC 65-15)

Also known as a ground proximity switch or landing gear "squat" switch, this switch is usually mounted in a bracket on one of the main gear shock struts and mechanically actuated via the landing gear torque links. The torque links spread apart or move together as the shock strut piston extends or retracts in its cylinder. When the strut is compressed (aircraft on the ground), the torque links are close together, causing the adjusting links to open the safety switch. During takeoff, as the weight of the aircraft leaves the struts, the struts and torque links extend causing the adjusting links to close the safety switch. A ground is completed when the safety switch closes and the solenoid then energizes, unlocking the selector valve so that the gear handle can be positioned to raise the gear. Squat switches also provide signals to other various aircraft systems indicating whether the aircraft is in the air or on the ground such as pressurization, nose wheel steering, thrust reversers, APU, etc.

4. What is a brake anti-skid system? (AC 65-15)

A system in high-performance aircraft braking systems that provides anti-skid protection and subsequent maximum braking efficiency. Anti-skid system sensors monitor and compare wheel rotation speed to the expected value on a dry runway. Once the system detects a rotational value less than normal, a skid control valve removes some of the hydraulic pressure to the wheel, permitting the wheel to rotate a little faster and stop its sliding. The more intense the skid is, the more braking pressure is removed. The skid detection and control of each wheel is completely independent of the others. The wheel skid intensity is measured by the amount of wheel slow down.

5. What other functions are provided by an anti-skid system? (AC 65-15)

a. *Touchdown protection*—this circuit prevents the brakes from being applied during the landing approach, even if the brake pedals are depressed. This prevents the wheels from being locked when they contact the runway.

b. *Fail-safe protection*—this circuit monitors operation of the skid control system. It automatically returns the brake system to full manual in case of system failure.

G. Pneumatic

1. What are some of the common components found in most pneumatic systems? (AC 65-15)

a. *Relief valves*—used in pneumatic systems to prevent damage. They act as pressure-limiting units and prevent excessive pressures from bursting lines and blowing out seals.

b. *Control valves*—controls the direction and amount of flow.

c. *Check valves*—a one-direction flow control valve.

d. *Restrictors*—are a type of control valve which reduces the rate of airflow and the speed of operation of an actuating unit.

e. *Filters*—protect pneumatic systems against dirt.

2. What is bleed air? (AC 65-12A)

Bleed air is taken from any of the various pressure stages of a compressor. The exact location of the bleed ports is, of course, dependent on the pressure or temperature required for a particular job. The ports are small openings in the compressor case adjacent to the particular stage from which the air is to be bled; thus, varying degrees of pressure or heat are available simply by tapping into the appropriate stage (i.e., P 2.5 or P 3.0 air). Air is often bled from the final or highest pressure stage, since at this point, pressure and air temperature are at a maximum. At times it may be necessary to cool this high pressure air. If it is used for cabin pressurization or other purposes where excess heat would be uncomfortable or detrimental, the air is sent through a refrigeration unit.

3. Which systems use bleed air? (AC 65-12A)

Bleed air is utilized in a wide variety of ways depending on the aircraft. Some of the most common applications are:

a. Cabin pressurization, heating, and cooling.

b. Deicing and anti-icing equipment.

c. Power for running instruments.

d. Pressurization of hydraulic reservoirs.

e. Auxiliary drive units (ADU).

f. Control booster servo-systems.

g. Pneumatic starting of engines.

4. **What are some operational considerations for aircraft equipped with a bleed air system?**

The available amount of power produced by an engine is reduced with the use of bleed air, since air pressure and heat are extracted from the compressors prior to combustion.

Restrictions are imposed concerning the use of bleed air during takeoffs and maximum performance situations, such as go-arounds. When use of bleed air during takeoff is necessary (i.e., operation of deice or anti-ice equipment in icing conditions), correction factors are applied restricting takeoff speeds and weights.

Leaks that develop in the bleed air ducting can result in onboard fires due to the extremely high operating temperatures. Bleed air systems use a system of sensors located along the various ducts to alert pilots of bleed air leaks or over-temperature conditions.

5. **What is an APU?**

An "auxiliary power unit" is a gas turbine powered engine used to provide a supplementary source of pneumatic and electrical power to the aircraft, usually located in the aft fuselage and isolated from the rest of the airplane by a firewall. An APU can be used simultaneously with or independently from the other airplane power sources, and are normally used to operate aircraft systems while on the ground. However, they may also be used in-flight as a source of backup electrical power for the main generators, as well as pneumatic power for in-flight pressurization and air conditioning systems.

H. Environmental

1. **What are the two most common air-cooling systems utilized in turbine-powered aircraft?** (AC 65-15)

a. Air-cycle machine.

b. Vapor-cycle machine.

2. What is an air-cycle machine (ACM)? (AC 65-15A)

It is a type of cooling system used mainly in larger turbine-powered aircraft, consisting of an expansion turbine (cooling turbine), an air-to-air heat exchanger, and valves that control airflow through the system. The expansion turbine incorporates an impeller and a turbine on a common shaft. High-pressure air from the compressor is routed through the turbine section; as the air passes through the turbine, it rotates the turbine and the impeller. After the compressed air performs the work of turning the turbine, it undergoes a pressure and temperature drop. It is this temperature drop that produces the cold air used for air conditioning.

3. Discuss the operational cycle of a typical ACM.

Bleed air is fed to a primary heat exchanger; the bleed air passing through the heat exchanger is cooled by ground air (driven by cooling fans) or ram air (in-flight). Heat exchangers are similar in design to radiators. The cooled bleed air is then routed to a turbine-driven compressor.

The compressor compresses the cooled air resulting in an increase in temperature. The compressed air is then routed to a secondary heat exchanger where the air is again cooled. A water separator removes water vapor, which is then used to provide additional cooling for the heat exchanger.

The compressed, dry air is then routed to drive a turbine where it is also expanded and, therefore cooled again (near 0°C at this point). Depending on the temperature selected, cold air is mixed with hot air in a mixing chamber and then supplied to the cabin/cockpit areas by recirculation fans.

4. What is a vapor-cycle machine (VCM)? (AC 65-15A)

A type of cooling system used mostly in smaller aircraft, or aircraft with a limited supply of bleed air (smaller engines). VCMs are similar in principle to the kitchen refrigerator or air conditioner in a car. They use similar components and operating principles, and in most cases depend upon an electrical system for power. This system usually has a greater cooling capacity than an air-cycle system, and in addition, can usually be used for cooling on the ground when the engines are not operating. These systems are also used on several large transport category type of aircraft.

5. What are the major components of a vapor-cycle machine? (AC 65-15A)

The compressor, condenser, evaporator, and expansion valve. Other minor items may include the condenser fan, receiver (refrigerated gas storage), dryer, surge valve, and temperature controls. These items are interconnected by appropriate tubing to form a closed loop in which the refrigerated gas is circulated during operation.

6. Discuss the operational cycle of a typical VCM. (AC 65-15A)

a. *Compressor*—increases the pressure of refrigerated gas when in vapor form. This high pressure raises the condensation temperature of the gas and produces the force necessary to circulate the gas through the system. The compressor is driven either by an electric motor or air-turbine drive mechanism.

b. *Condenser*—refrigerated gas is pumped to the condenser for the next step in the cycle. At the condenser, the gas goes through a heat exchanger where outside (ambient) air removes heat from it. When heat is removed from the high-pressure gas, its state changes and it condenses to a liquid, releasing the heat the gas picked up from the cabin air.

c. *Receiver*—From the condenser, the liquid gas flows to the receiver which acts as a reservoir for the liquid refrigerant. The fluid level in the receiver varies with system demands. During peak cooling periods, there will be less liquid than when the load is light. The prime function of the receiver is to ensure that the thermostatic expansion valve is not starved for refrigerant under heavy cooling load conditions.

d. *Evaporator*—Some vapor-cycle systems use an evaporator or subcooler to reduce the temperature of the liquid refrigerant after it leaves the receiver. By cooling the refrigerant, premature vaporization (flash-off) can be prevented. Maximum cooling takes place when the refrigerant changes from a liquid to a gaseous state. Air routed past the evaporator is cooled and recirculated to the cabin/cockpit areas.

7. Describe the function of a heat exchanger. (AC 65-15A)

A heat exchanger is a device that transfers heat between two different fluids. When two fluids of different temperatures come into contact, heat transfer occurs from the hotter to the cooler. Heat exchangers apply this principle of temperature control in a variety of systems of turbine aircraft, such as in fuel heaters, oil coolers and air conditioning systems.

I. Pressurization

1. What are several functions that must be accomplished by a cabin pressurization system? (AC 65-15A)

It must be capable of maintaining a cabin pressure altitude of approximately 8,000 feet at the aircraft's maximum designed cruising altitude. The system must also be designed to prevent rapid changes of cabin altitude that may be uncomfortable or injurious to passengers and crew. The pressurization system should permit a reasonably fast exchange of air from inside to outside the cabin, in order to eliminate odors and remove stale air.

2. What areas are pressurized in most turbine-powered aircraft? (AC 65-15A)

In the typical pressurization system, the cabin, flight compartment, and baggage compartments are incorporated into a sealed unit capable of containing air under a pressure higher than outside atmospheric pressure.

3. Describe in general terms how the cabin pressurization system functions. (AC 65-15A)

Pressurized air is pumped into a sealed fuselage through use of engine bleed air, which provides a relatively constant volume of air at all altitudes up to a designed maximum. Air is released from the fuselage by a device called an outflow valve. Since a relatively constant inflow of bleed air is provided to the pressurized area, the outflow valve, by regulating the air exit, is the major controlling element in the pressurization system.

4. What is a pressurization controller? (AC 65-15A)

The pressurization controller is the source of control signals for the pressurization system. The controller automatically (or manually) controls the outflow valves to maintain the desired pressurization level, and provides several adjustment knobs to obtain the desired type of pressurized condition.

5. Describe the various pressurization controller indicators. (AC 65-15A)

a. *Cabin differential pressure gauge* — indicates the difference between inside and outside pressure. This gauge should be monitored to ensure the cabin is not approaching the maximum allowable differential pressure.

b. *Cabin altimeter* — indicates cabin pressure altitude. Provides a check on system performance; in some cases the cabin altimeter indicator may be incorporated into the cabin differential pressure gauge indicator, thus eliminating the need for two separate gauges.

c. *Cabin rate-of-climb or descent* — indicates cabin rate-of-climb.

6. What are outflow valves? (AC 65-15A)

The principal control of the pressurization system is the outflow valve. Cabin pressure is maintained by manually or automatically regulating the amount of cabin air vented overboard by the outflow valve(s), which is placed in a pressurized portion of the fuselage, usually underneath the lower compartments. The flow through an outflow valve is determined by the degree of valve opening, ordinarily controlled by an automatic system that can be set by the flight crewmembers.

7. Discuss the operation of outflow valves on the ground and in the air. (AC 65-15A)

In many aircraft, the outflow valve(s) will be held fully open on the ground by a landing gear operated switch. During flight, as altitude is gained, the valve(s) close(s) gradually to make a greater restriction to the outflow of cabin air. The cabin rate-of-climb or descent is determined by the rate of closing or opening of the outflow valve(s). During cruising flight the cabin altitude is directly related to the degree of outflow valve opening.

8. Define "cabin differential pressure." (AC 65-15A)

Cabin differential pressure is the ratio between inside and outside air pressures and is a measure of the internal stress on the fuselage skin. If the differential pressure becomes too great, structural damage to the fuselage may occur.

9. What are negative pressure-relief valves? (AC 65-15A)

All pressurized aircraft require some form of a negative pressure-relief valve. This valve may also be incorporated into the outflow valve or may be an individual unit. A common form of negative pressure-relief valve is a simple hinged flap on the rear wall (pressure dome) of the cabin. This valve opens when outside air pressure is greater than cabin pressure. During pressurized flight, the internal cabin pressure holds the flap closed and the negative pressure-relief valve prevents cabin altitude from accidentally going higher than the aircraft altitude.

10. What is a dump valve? (AC 65-15A)

Also known as a safety-relief or manual depressurization valve. A manually operated valve for controlling pressurization when all other means of control have failed. Permits rapid depressurization during fires or an emergency descent.

11. What are positive pressure-relief valves? (AC 65-15A)

Also known as an automatic cabin-pressure relief valve, these are used on all pressurized aircraft. May actually be built into the outflow valve or may be an entirely separate unit. The pressure-relief valve automatically opens when the cabin differential pressure reaches a preset value.

J. Fire Protection

1. What are the subsystems of the fire protection system in most large turbine engine aircraft? (AC 65-15A)

a. Fire detection system.

b. Fire extinguishing system.

2. What areas within an aircraft are normally provided with fire detection and/or fire extinguishing capability? (AC 65-15A)

a. Engine and nacelle areas.

b. Wheel wells (brake fires).

c. Cargo and lavatory compartments.

d. Bleed air ducting areas.

e. APU compartment.

3. What are the different types of aircraft fire detection systems in common use? (AC 65-15A)

a. *Thermal switch system*—heat-sensitive units that complete electrical circuits at a certain temperature. If the temperature rises above a set value in any section of the circuit, the thermal switch will close, completing the light circuit to indicate the presence of a fire or overheat condition.

b. *Thermocouple system*—depends upon rate of temperature rise; compares the rate of temperature rise of an unprotected thermocouple to a protected thermocouple. If the temperature rises rapidly, the thermocouple produces a voltage due to the temperature difference between the two. If both are heated at the same rate, no voltage will result and no warning signal is given.

c. *Continuous-loop detector system*—also called a sensing system, permits more complete coverage of a fire hazard area than any spot-type temperature detectors. Continuous-loop systems are versions of the thermal switch system. They are overheat systems with heat sensitive units that complete electrical circuits at a certain temperature. There is no rate of heat rise sensitivity in a continuous-loop system.

4. What is the function of a fire "T" handle? (AC 65-15A)

Also known as a fire-pull handle; a fire "T" handle is a very important handle found in an aircraft cockpit, usually located on the instrument panel, glare shield, or fire control panel. The handle, when pulled, will actuate micro switches that energize and close various valves such as the emergency fuel shutoff valve, hydraulic shutoff valve, and engine bleed-air valve. Pulling the T-handle will also arm a fire-extinguishing agent, activate an electric feathering mechanism, and disconnect the generator from the electrical system. A "T" handle may contain a fire warning light for each engine, located within the handle itself.

5. How is fire extinguishing accomplished? (AC 65-15A)

The typical fire-extinguishing portion of a complete fire protection system consists of remotely actuated cylinders or containers of extinguishing agent for each engine and nacelle area. One type of installation provides for a container in each of four pylons on a multi-engine aircraft. The extinguishing agent container is equipped with two discharge valves operated by electrically discharged cartridges. These two valves are the main and the reserve controls that release and route the agent to the pod and pylon in which the container is located, or to the other engine on the same wing. This type of two-shot, crossfeed configuration permits the release of a second charge of fire-extinguishing agent to the same engine if another fire breaks out, without providing two containers for each engine area.

6. What is "PBE"?

Protective Breathing Equipment is used in the event of smoke and fire and protects the entire head and shoulders of the person wearing it. Contains an oxygen generator which makes it a totally self-contained unit. Required by 14 CFR Part 121 regulations.

K. Ice Protection

1. What are several methods to prevent or control ice formation on aircraft? (AC 65-15A)

a. *Thermal*—heating surfaces using hot air.

b. *Electrical*—heating by electrical elements.

c. *Pneumatic*—breaking up ice formations, usually by inflatable boots.

d. *Alcohol*—use of alcohol spray.

2. How do deice boots work? (AC 65-15A)

Pneumatic deicing systems use rubber deicers, called boots or shoes, attached to the leading edge of the wing and stabilizers. The deicers are composed of a series of inflatable tubes, which during operation, are inflated with pressurized air and deflated in an alternating cycle. This inflation and deflation causes the ice to crack and break off. The ice is then carried away by the airstream. Deicer tubes are inflated by an engine-driven air pump (vacuum pump), or by air bled from gas turbine engine compressors. The inflation sequence is controlled by either a centrally-located distributor valve, or by solenoid-operated valves located adjacent to the deicer air inlets.

3. How do leading edge anti-ice systems work? (AC 65-15A)

Thermal systems used for the purpose of preventing the formation of ice use heated air ducted span-wise along the inside of the leading edge of the airfoil and distributed around its inner surface. There are several methods used to provide heated air. These include bleeding hot air from the turbine compressor, engine exhaust heat exchangers, and ram air heated by a combustion heater. Some aircraft systems include an automatic temperature control, in which temperature is maintained within a predetermined range by mixing heated air with cold air. A system of valves is provided in some installations to enable certain parts of the anti-icing system to be shut off. In the event of an engine failure, these valves also permit supplying the entire anti-icing system with heated air from one or more of the remaining engines.

4. What system is used for propeller anti-icing?
(AC 65-12A)

Most turboprop aircraft utilize a "hot prop" system which consists of an electrical energy source, a resistance heating element, system controls, and necessary wiring. The heating elements are mounted internally or externally on the propeller spinner and blades. Electrical power from the aircraft system is transferred to the propeller hub through electrical leads, which terminate in slip rings and brushes. Flexible connectors are used to transfer power from the hub to the blade elements. Icing control is accomplished by converting electrical energy to heat energy in the heating element. An automatic timer is used to control the sequence and operation of heating current in the blade elements.

5. What methods are used to prevent ice from forming in the engine air inlet? (AFM)

An engine inlet anti-ice system prevents ice from forming in the induction system via methods such as high-pressure bleed air, and electrically-heated elements. In some aircraft, hot exhaust air may be utilized. These systems are mounted on the engine nacelle air inlet lip, as well as in the forward area of the inertial separator (S-shaped duct). Some systems have a timer that automatically activates and deactivates the system, while other systems are operational from engine start to engine shut down.

6. What is an inertial separator? (AFM)

An S-shaped duct in the induction system of a turboprop engine that separates incoming air from suspended particles of ice, dirt, birds, etc., by forcing the incoming air to turn before entering the engine. Since foreign objects are solid they tend to continue in a straight line and most are separated by inertia at these bend points.

7. What other aircraft surfaces are provided with icing protection? What type of protection? (AC 65-15A)

Leading edges of vertical and horizontal stabilizers—pneumatic, thermal

Windshields, windows, and radomes—electrical, alcohol

Stall warning transmitters—electrical

Pitot tubes—electrical

Angle-of-attack sensors—electrical

Total air temperature sensors—electrical

Flight controls—pneumatic, thermal

Lavatory drains—electrical

Landing gear—thermal

L. Flight Controls

1. What are examples of primary and secondary/auxiliary flight controls? (FAA-H-8083-25)

Primary—Ailerons, elevators, and rudder

Secondary/Auxiliary—Trim tabs, balance tabs, servo tabs, flaps, spoilers and leading edge devices

2. What are trim tabs? (AC 65-15A)

Trim tabs trim the aircraft in flight; that is, they correct any tendency of the aircraft to move toward an undesirable flight attitude. They control aircraft balance so that the aircraft maintains straight-and-level flight without pressure on the control column, control wheel, or rudder pedals. Movement of the tab in one direction causes a deflection of the control surface in the opposite direction. Most of the trim tabs installed on aircraft are mechanically operated from the cockpit through an individual cable system; some aircraft have trim tabs operated by an electrical actuator. Trim tabs are installed on elevators, rudders, and ailerons.

3. What is the function of a servo tab? (AC 65-15A)

Servo tabs are very similar in operation and appearance to the trim tabs. Sometimes referred to as flight tabs, they are used primarily on the large main control surfaces to aid in moving the control surface and holding it in the desired position. Only the servo tab moves in response to movement of the cockpit control. The force of the airflow on the servo tab then moves the primary control surface. Less force is needed to move the main control surface when servo tabs are used.

4. What is the function of leading edge flaps? (AC 65-15A)

Leading edge flaps are airfoils extended from and retracted into the leading edge of the wing, used principally on large high-speed aircraft. When they are in the "up" (retracted) position, they fair in with the wings and serve as part of the wing trailing edge. When in the "down" (extended) position, the flaps pivot on the hinge points and drop to about a 45° or 50° angle with the wing chord line. This increases the wing camber and changes the airflow, providing greater lift.

5. What is flap asymmetry?

Flap asymmetry is when the flap position varies within a pair of flaps.

6. What are ground spoilers? (AC 65-15A)

Ground spoilers are lift-decreasing devices that are extended only after the aircraft is on the ground. They assist in braking action.

7. What are flight spoilers? (AC 65-15A)

Flight spoilers are auxiliary wing flight control surfaces, mounted on the upper surface of each wing, that operate in conjunction with the ailerons to provide lateral control. A wing's flight spoiler assists in lateral control by extending whenever the aileron is rotated up. When actuated as speed brakes, the spoiler panels on both wings raise up—the panel on the "up" aileron wing raises more than the panel on the "down" aileron side. This provides speed brake operation and lateral control simultaneously. The purpose of the spoilers is to disturb the smooth airflow across the top of the airfoil, thereby creating an increased amount of drag and a decreased amount of lift on that airfoil.

8. What are speed brakes? (AC 65-15A)

Speed brakes, sometimes called dive flaps or dive brakes, serve to slow an aircraft in flight. These brakes are used when descending at a steep angle or when approaching the runway for a landing. Speed brakes are designed to create drag without affecting lift.

9. What are leading edge slats? (AC 65-15A)

A slat is a movable control surface attached to the leading edge of a wing. When the slat is closed, (low angle-of-attack, high airspeed) it forms the leading edge of the wing. When in the open position (high angle-of-attack, low airspeed) the slat is extended forward, creating a slot between the slat and the wing leading edge. This increases the wing camber and changes the airflow, providing greater lift and allowing the aircraft to be controlled at airspeeds below the otherwise normal landing speed.

10. What are slots? (FAA-H-8083-30)

A slot in the leading edge of a wing directs high-energy air from under the wing to the airflow above the wing, accelerating upper airflow. By accelerating the airflow above the wing, airflow separation will be delayed to higher angles of attack. This allows the wing to continue to develop lift at substantially higher angles of attack.

11. What are stabilons?

Small, horizontal, wing-like flight surfaces mounted on both sides of the fuselage, below the T-tail, designed to improve longitudinal (pitch) stability of the aircraft and provide better stall recovery characteristics.

12. What are tailets?

Small vertical fins mounted to the lower sides of the horizontal stabilizer tips, designed to improve directional stability.

13. What is a vortex generator? (AC 65-15A)

A vortex generator is a complementary pair of small, low-aspect-ratio (short span in relation to chord) airfoils mounted at opposite angles of attack to each other and perpendicular to the aerodynamic surface they serve. The airfoils of the generator develop lift, and with their low aspect ratio also develop very strong tip vortices. These tip vortices cause air to flow outward and inward in circular paths around the ends of the airfoils. The vortices generated have the effect of drawing high-energy air from outside the boundary layer into the slower moving air close to the skin of the aerodynamic surface.

14. Describe the function of vortex generators attached to the following aircraft structures: wing, vertical stabilizer, horizontal stabilizer. (AC 65-15A)

a. Wing (upper surface)—delay the onset of drag divergence at high speeds and also aid in maintaining aileron effectiveness at high speeds.

b. Vertical stabilizer (both sides)—prevent flow separation over the rudder during extreme angles of yaw after an engine loss at very low speeds.

c. Horizontal stabilizer (upper and lower surface)—prevents flow separation over the elevators at very low speeds.

In summary, vortex generators on wing surfaces improve high-speed characteristics, while vortex generators on tail surfaces generally improve low-speed characteristics.

M. Warning and Emergency Systems

1. What is an aural warning system? (AC 65-15A)

This system alerts the flight crew of an unsafe condition. A typical transport aircraft's aural warning system will alert the pilot with audio and voice signals of conditions including: an abnormal takeoff condition, landing condition, pressurization condition, mach speed condition, an engine or wheel-well fire, calls from the crew call system, etc. These systems are necessary for the safe operation of the most complex transport aircraft.

2. Discuss the function of an annunciator system.
(AC 65-15A)

Complex turbine aircraft are equipped with annunciator systems that allow a pilot to monitor multiple aircraft systems in one centralized display. An annunciator panel provides indication to the pilot of system status, abnormalities and emergencies. The panel is usually centrally located in the cockpit and consists of three types of annunciators: warning, caution, and advisory.

3. What color are warning, caution, and advisory lights, and what action is required if illuminated?

Warning—Red; indicates an unsatisfactory condition; emergency requiring immediate action.

Caution—Amber; indicates a caution/borderline condition; usually a malfunction requiring action as soon as possible.

Advisory—Green; indicates a satisfactory or normal operation; no action required.

4. What is a "master caution light"? (AC 65-15A)

Certain system failures are immediately indicated on an annunciator panel on the main instrument panel. A "master caution light" and a light indicating the faulting system flash "On." The master light may be reset to "Off," but the indicating light will remain "On" until the fault is corrected or the equipment concerned is shut down. By resetting, the master caution light is ready to warn of a subsequent fault even before correction of the initial fault. A press-to-test light is available for testing the circuits in this system.

5. What is the purpose of stick shaker and stick pusher systems? (FAA-H-8083-3)

On airplanes susceptible to deep stalls (some swept and/or tapered wing airplanes), sophisticated stall warning systems such as stick shakers and stick pushers are standard equipment. A stick shaker is an artificial stall warning device that vibrates the control column, normally activating around 107 percent of the actual stall speed. A stick pusher is a device that automatically applies an abrupt and large forward force on the control column when the airplane is nearing an angle of attack where a stall could occur.

N. Advanced Avionics

1. Describe the function of the following avionics equipment acronyms: AHRS, ADC, PFD, MFD, FD, FMS, INS. (FAA-H-8083-6)

AHRS—Attitude and Heading Reference System: composed of three-axis sensors that provide heading, attitude, and yaw information for aircraft. AHRS are designed to replace traditional mechanical gyroscopic flight instruments and provide superior reliability and accuracy.

ADC—Air Data Computer: an aircraft computer that receives and processes pitot pressure, static pressure, and temperature to calculate very precise altitude, indicated airspeed, true airspeed, vertical speed and air temperature.

PFD—Primary Flight Display: a display that provides increased situational awareness to the pilot by replacing the traditional six instruments with an easy-to-scan lay-out of horizon, airspeed, altitude, vertical speed, trend, trim, rate-of-turn, among other key indications.

MFD—Multi Function Display: a cockpit display capable of presenting information (navigation data, moving maps, terrain awareness, etc.) to the pilot in numerous configurable ways; often used in concert with the PFD.

FD—Flight Director: an electronic flight computer that analyzes the navigation selections, signals, and aircraft parameters, presented as steering instructions on the flight display with command bars or crossbars for the pilot to position the nose of the aircraft over or follow.

FMS—Flight Management System: a computer system containing a database to allow programming of routes, approaches, and departures that can supply navigation data to the flight director/autopilot from various sources. Calculates flight data such as fuel consumption, time remaining, possible range, and other values.

INS—Inertial Navigation System: a self-contained navigation system using sensors to measure changes in motion of aircraft, acceleration and deceleration, airspeed, altitude, and heading to maintain current position of aircraft. Also called "position keeping" because an interruption of the system requires the pilot to initialize or enter the beginning point of aircraft position reference.

2. What is the function of a magnetometer? (FAA-H-8083-6)

A magnetometer is a device that measures the strength of the earth's magnetic field to determine aircraft heading. It provides this information digitally to the AHRS, which relays it to the PFD.

3. When powering up an aircraft with a FMS/RNAV unit installed, how will you verify the effective dates of the navigation database? (FAA-H-8083-6)

The effective dates for the navigation database are typically shown on a start-up screen that is displayed as the system cycles through its startup self-test.

4. How often are updates available for GPS airborne navigation databases? (AC 90-94)

Waypoint information is provided and maintained by the National Flight Data Center (NFDC). The data is typically updated at regular intervals, such as the internationally agreed upon Aeronautical Information Regulation and Control (AIRAC) cycle of every 28 days.

5. Does an aircraft have to remain stationary during AHRS system initialization? (FAA-H-8083-6)

Some AHRSs must be initialized on the ground prior to departure. The initialization procedure allows the system to establish a reference attitude used as a benchmark for all future attitude changes. Other systems are capable of initialization while taxiing as well as in-flight.

6. Which standby flight instruments are normally provided in an advanced avionics aircraft? (FAA-H-8083-6)

Every aircraft equipped with electronic flight instruments must also contain a minimal set of backup/standby instruments. Usually conventional "round dial instruments," they typically include an attitude indicator, an airspeed indicator, and an altimeter.

7. If one display fails (PFD or MFD), what information will be presented on the remaining display? (FAA-H-8083-6)

In the event of a display failure, some systems offer a reversion capability to display the primary flight instruments/engine instruments on the remaining operative display.

8. When a display failure occurs, what other system components will be affected? (AFM/POH)

In some systems, failure of a display will also result in partial loss of navigation, communication and GPS capability.

9. What display information will be affected when an ADC failure occurs? (FAA-H-8083-6)

Inoperative airspeed, altitude, and vertical speed indicators (red Xs) on the PFD indicate the failure of the air data computer.

10. What display information will be lost when an AHRS failure occurs? (FAA-H-8083-6)

An inoperative attitude indicator (red X) on a PFD indicates failure of the AHRS.

11. How will loss of a magnetometer affect the AHRS operation? (FAA-H-8083-6)

Heading information will be lost.

12. Give a brief description of an automated flight control system in a technically advanced aircraft. (FAA-H-8083-6)

Most automated flight control systems are two different, but integrated systems:

Autopilot—set of servo actuators that do the control movement and the control circuits to make the servo actuators move the correct amount for the selected task; manipulates the roll, pitch, and, in some cases, the yaw control surfaces of the airplane.

Flight Director—the brain of the autopilot system; while most autopilots can fly straight and level, the additional tasks of finding a selected course (intercepting), changing altitudes, and tracking navigation sources with cross winds, etc. are handled by the flight director.

13. Describe several methods for disconnecting a malfunctioning autopilot. (FAA-H-8083-6)

a. Autopilot disconnect switch (typically mounted on control yoke).

b. Mode buttons on the autopilot control panel.

c. Circuit breakers that interrupt power to the autopilot/trim systems.

d. Overpowering the system by forcing the control yoke in the desired direction.

14. What is the Traffic Information Service (TIS)? (FAA-H-8083-6)

TIS captures traffic information that appears on radar scopes at nearby ATC facilities and broadcasts that information to appropriately equipped aircraft. Aircraft must be equipped with a transponder capable of receiving TIS broadcasts. TIS-capable aircraft can observe traffic information in the cockpit and receive traffic advisories for proximate aircraft.

15. Explain the limitations a pilot should be aware of when using TIS. (FAA-H-8083-6, AIM 4-4-17)

a. TIS data is only transmitted from approach radar facilities; no information is broadcast from en route (ARTCC) facilities. Some approach radar facilities are not equipped to send TIS information.

b. The aircraft must be within range (approximately 50 NM) and within line-of-site of the TIS station to receive broadcasts.

c. TIS does not respond to aircraft that are not transponder equipped, aircraft with a transponder failure, or aircraft out of radar coverage.

d. TIS alone does not ensure safe separation in every case.

16. Briefly describe the Terrain Awareness and Warning System (TAWS). (FAA-H-8083-6)

TAWS uses the aircraft's GPS navigation signal and altimetry systems to compare the position and trajectory of the aircraft against a more detailed terrain and obstacle database. This database attempts to detail every obstruction that could pose a threat to an aircraft in flight. There are two classes of certified TAWS that differ in the capabilities they provide to the pilot: TAWS A and TAWS B.

17. What is a Doppler Radar navigation system? (AIM 1-1-18)

Doppler Radar is a semi-automatic self-contained dead reckoning navigation system (radar sensor plus computer) that is not continuously dependent on information from ground based or external aids. Radar signals detect and measure ground speed and drift angle, using the aircraft compass system as its directional reference.

Performance

2

A. Takeoff and Climb

1. **Depending on the specific rule under which an airplane was certified, what are examples of calculations that must be performed to determine the allowable takeoff weight?** (Order 8900.1)

    a. AFM maximum weight limitations (structural) — takeoff, zero fuel, landing

    b. Airport elevation and temperature — departure point, destination, alternate

    c. Runway limit weight — accelerate-stop distance, accelerate-go (one engine inoperative), all-engines takeoff distance

    d. Takeoff climb limit weight — first segment, second segment, transition segment (divided into third and fourth segments under some rules)

    e. Takeoff obstacle limit weight

    f. Enroute climb limit and terrain clearance weights — all engines operative, one engine inoperative, two engines inoperative

    g. Approach climb limit weight

    h. Landing climb limit weight

    i. Destination landing distance weight

    j. Alternate landing distance weight

2. **What does the term "takeoff climb limit weight" mean?** (Order 8900.1)

    The weight at which the airplane can climb at a specified minimum climb gradient or specified minimum climb rate in still air through the segments of the takeoff flight path. Climb performance for turbine-powered transport category and commuter category airplanes is measured in terms of a gradient (percent of height gained divided by distance traveled) in specified climb segments.

3. **What are several factors that determine the usable runway length available for takeoff?** (Order 8900.1)

    The usable runway length may be shorter or longer than the actual runway length due to stopways, clearways, and obstacle clearance planes.

4. What is the rule concerning required takeoff distances for transport or commuter category aircraft?
(Order 8900.1)

The required takeoff distance is the longest of three takeoff distances: accelerate-stop, accelerate-go, and all-engines. Since the available runway length is a fixed value, allowable takeoff weight for any given runway is determined by the most restrictive of the applicable distances.

5. Define the term "accelerate-stop takeoff distance."
(Order 8900.1)

The total distance required to perform the following actions:

a. With all engines operating at takeoff thrust, accelerate from a standing start to V_{EF} (engine failure) speed at which the critical engine is assumed to fail;

b. Make the transition from takeoff thrust to idle thrust, extend spoilers or other drag devices, and apply wheel brakes;

c. Decelerate and bring the airplane to a full stop.

6. Define the term "accelerate-go takeoff distance."
(Order 8900.1)

The accelerate-go (with one engine inoperative) takeoff distance is the total distance required to perform the following actions:

a. With all engines operating, accelerate to V_{EF} speed with the flightcrew's recognition of the failure at V_1;

b. With one engine inoperative, continue acceleration to V_R speed at which time the nosegear is raised off the ground;

c. Climb to the specified runway crossing height (RCH) and cross it at V_2 speed.

7. Define the term "all-engines takeoff distance."
(Order 8900.1)

All-engines takeoff distance is the total distance required, with all engines at takeoff thrust, to accelerate to V_R or V_2 speed (appropriate to the airplane type) and rotate and climb to a specified RCH.

8. What is the definition of "balanced field length"?
(AC 120-62)

The runway length (or runway plus clearway and/or stopway)
where, for takeoff weight, the engine-out accelerate-go distance
equals the accelerate-stop distance.

9. Define the term "critical field length." (AC 120-62)

The minimum runway length (or runway plus clearway and/or
stopway) required for a specific takeoff weight. This distance may
be the longer of the balanced field length, 115% of the all engine
takeoff distance, or established by other limitations such as maintaining V_1 to be less than or equal to V_R.

**10. What factors should be taken into consideration when
computing takeoff performance?** (Order 8900.1)

a. Airport elevation
b. Temperature
c. Density altitude
d. Weight
e. Flap selection
f. Runway slope
g. Wind conditions
h. Water and contamination of runway
i. Tire speed and brake limits

11. How does airport elevation affect takeoff performance?
(Order 8900.1)

Airport elevation is accounted for in takeoff computations because
the true airspeed (ground speed in no-wind conditions) for a given
takeoff increases as air density decreases. As airport elevation
increases, the takeoff run required before the airplane reaches V_1,
V_{LOF}, and V_2 speeds increases; the stopping distance from V_1
increases; and a greater air distance is traversed from liftoff to the
specified RCH because of the increased true airspeed at the indicated V_2 speed.

12. How does temperature affect takeoff performance?
(Order 8900.1)

As air temperature increases, airplane performance is adversely affected because of a reduction in air density. Less dense air causes a reduction in attainable takeoff thrust and aerodynamic performance.

13. How does density altitude affect takeoff performance?
(Order 8900.1)

Takeoff performance is usually depicted in an AFM for various elevations and temperatures. The effect of variations in barometric pressure is not usually computed or required by the regulations. However, some airplanes with specific engine installations must have corrections in allowable weight for lower-than-standard barometric pressure.

14. How does weight affect takeoff performance?
(Order 8900.1)

Increasing takeoff weight increases the following:

a. V_{LOF} and the ground run distance required to reach the liftoff point.

b. The air distance required to travel from the liftoff point to the specified runway crossing height.

c. The distance required to bring the aircraft to a stop from V_1 speed, and the energy absorbed by the brakes during the stop.

15. How does flap selection affect takeoff performance?
(Order 8900.1)

The effect of selecting more flap (within the allowable range) reduces V_R, V_{LOF}, and the required ground-run distance to reach liftoff. All of these increase the accelerate-stop distance limit weight, the accelerate-go distance limit weight, and the all-engines operating limit weight. The additional flap extension increases aerodynamic drag and also decreases the climb gradient the airplane can maintain past the end of the runway. In the case of a short runway, it may not be possible to take off without the flaps set at the greatest extension allowed for takeoff. In the case of a long runway, at a high elevation and a high ambient temperature, it may only be possible to climb at the required gradient with the minimum allowable takeoff flap extension.

16. How does runway slope affect takeoff performance?
(Order 8900.1)

Uphill grades increase the ground run required to reach the points at which V_1, V_R, and V_{LOF} are attained, but they also improve stopping distance. When climbing over an uphill grade runway you'll need more distance to reach the specified RCH. The reverse is true of downhill grades. Gradient corrections are computed for both runway length and takeoff speeds, and the average runway gradient (determined by dividing the difference in elevation of the two ends of the runway by the runway length) is normally used.

For large variations in runway height (±5 feet), the retarding effect on the uphill segment is proportionally greater than the acceleration gained on the downhill portion. In this case the slope used for computations should be proportionately greater than the average slope.

17. How do wind conditions affect takeoff performance?
(Order 8900.1)

The effect of wind on the aircraft's climb gradient is significant, with tailwinds decreasing the gradient and headwinds increasing it:

a. *Headwinds.* It is not required, but the distances may be used to compute performance; only 1/2 of the reported steady-state wind component (parallel to the runway) may be used.

b. *Tailwinds.* For a downwind takeoff or landing, at least 150% of the reported steady state tailwind component must be used to compute the performance effect. Most airplanes are certified for takeoff with not more than 10 knots of tailwind component, but some have been certified with higher limits. To use these, the operator must not be limited by the AFM and must be authorized by the operations specifications.

c. *Crosswinds.* The maximum gust velocity must be used in the most unfavorable direction for computing the effective crosswind component. Crosswind values in most AFMs are stated as "demonstrated values" rather than as limits.

18. **How does water and contamination of runways affect takeoff performance?** (Order 8900.1)

    AFM performance data is based on a dry runway. When a runway is contaminated by water, snow, or ice, charted AFM performance values will not be obtained. The manufacturer's guidance material has appropriate corrections for these conditions to apply to performance calculations.

    The wet-to-dry stopping distance ratio on a well-maintained, grooved, wet runway is usually around 1.15 to 1. Where the grooves are not maintained and rubber deposits are heavy, the stopping distance ratio could be as high as 1.9 to 1. On ungrooved runways, the stopping distance ratio is usually about 2 to 1.

    In the case of a runway with new pavement or where rubber deposits are present, the ratio could be as high as 4 to 1. Some newly surfaced asphalt runway surfaces can be extremely slippery when only slightly wet.

19. **How does tire speed and brake limits affect takeoff performance?** (Order 8900.1)

    Allowable takeoff weight may be limited by either tire speed limits or the ability of the brakes to absorb the heat energy generated during the stop. The energy the brakes must absorb during a stop increases by the square of the speed at which the brakes are applied.

    Accelerate-stop distances are determined with cold brakes. When brakes are hot, they may not be able to absorb the energy generated, and charted AFM stopping distances may not be achieved. The heat generated by the stop may cause the wheels or tires to fail. Short turnaround times and rejected takeoffs present a potential hazard in terms of heat buildup in tires and in brake assemblies.

20. **What is the definition of the symbol V_1?** (14 CFR Part 1)

    V_1 speed—"takeoff decision speed," the maximum speed in the takeoff at which the pilot must take action (e.g., apply brakes, reduce thrust, deploy speed brakes) to stop the airplane within the accelerate-stop distance. Also, the minimum speed in the takeoff following a failure of the critical engine at V_{EF} at which the pilot can continue the takeoff, and achieve the required height above the takeoff surface within the takeoff distance.

21. What is the definition of the symbol V_R and V_{LOF}? (Order 8900.1)

V_R—rotation speed, determined so that V_2 speed is reached before the aircraft reaches 35 feet above the runway surface.
V_{LOF}—the speed at which the aircraft becomes airborne.

22. What is the definition of the symbol V_2? (14 CFR Part 1)

V_2— "takeoff safety speed," a referenced airspeed obtained after liftoff at which the required one-engine inoperative climb performance can be achieved.

23. What are some of the factors that affect V_1?

a. Density altitude

b. Gross weight

c. Runway slope or gradient

d. Runway surface (slush on runway, etc.)

e. Brake anti-skid on or off

24. What is an engine-out climb gradient? (Order 8900.1)

Turbine-powered transport category and commuter category airplanes climb performance is measured in terms of a gradient (height gained divided by distance traveled expressed as a percent) in specified climb segments. In the event of an engine failure, large, turbine-powered airplanes must be capable of climbing at a specified gradient through each of the defined climb segments of the takeoff flight path.

25. What are the basic climb segments of the takeoff path of large turbine-powered airplanes? (Order 8900.1)

a. The first climb segment starts from liftoff to the point at which the landing gear is retracted, but not less than 35 feet above the runway. Depending on the particular regulation an aircraft was certified under, it must attain V_2 speed before exceeding 35 feet above the runway surface or attain V_2 speed as it leaves the ground.

Continued

b. The second climb segment starts when the gear is retracted or at 35 feet, whichever is later, and continues at V_2 until the selected acceleration height (not less than 400 feet above the runway).

c. The third and final climb segment starts at the acceleration height and continues until the transition to the enroute configuration is complete (not lower than 1,000 feet or 1,500 feet above the runway, depending on which regulation the aircraft was certified under).

26. What is the definition of "clearway"? (14 CFR Part 1)

An area beyond the runway, not less than 500 feet wide, centrally located about the extended centerline of the runway, and under the control of the airport authorities. The clearway is expressed in terms of a clearway plane, extending from the end of the runway with an upward slope not exceeding 1.25 percent, above which no object nor any terrain protrudes.

27. What is the definition of "stopway"? (14 CFR Part 1)

Stopway means an area beyond the takeoff runway, no less wide than the runway and centered upon the extended centerline of the runway, able to support the airplane during an aborted takeoff, without causing structural damage to the airplane, and designated by the airport authorities for use in decelerating the airplane during an aborted takeoff.

28. What is the most effective means of ensuring that adequate engine-out climb performance is achieved? (Order 8900.1)

By limiting the takeoff gross weight so that, considering fuel burn, the aircraft will be light enough to ensure the necessary performance. This is usually accomplished by restricting the amount of fuel and/or passengers or cargo that can be carried.

29. What are "TOLD" cards?

Takeoff and landing data cards, or "TOLD" cards provide a quick reference source for pilots to determine airspeeds such as V_1, V_R, V_2, and V_{REF}. Airspeeds are precalculated for a variety of configuration, weight, and temperature combinations.

30. What are airport analysis tables? (Order 8900.1)

AFM data may be combined with airport and runway data, then published in tabular format. This airport analysis data is provided to flight crews (usually in the form of an approved manual) and contains performance data on all runways of operation at all airports the carrier is approved to operate from. Data includes: maximum allowable takeoff weight, climb limit weight, penalties for rolling takeoffs and intersection takeoffs, preferred takeoff profiles, etc. Runway analysis tables provide an easier method for calculating required performance for an authorized runway under specific conditions. The data is based on pertinent variables such as temperature, weight, thrust, runway condition and obstacles. Current airport analysis data is required to be on board the aircraft for every flight.

31. What are several examples of performance charts used for takeoff and climb data? (AFM)

a. Minimum takeoff power
b. Maximum takeoff weight
c. Takeoff distance
d. Accelerate-stop
e. Accelerate-go distance
f. Net gradient of climb one engine inoperative
g. Rate-of-climb two engines
h. Rate-of-climb one engine
i. Service ceiling one engine inoperative
j. Time, fuel, distance to cruise/climb
k. Performance climb—time, fuel, distance

B. Cruise

1. Define the term "specific range." (FAA-H-8083-25)

Specific range refers to the number of nautical air miles of flying distance per pound of fuel burned. Due to the relatively high fuel flows present in most turboprop and jet aircraft, the specific range is usually stated in nautical air miles flown per 100 lbs or 1,000 lbs of fuel burned.

2. How would you obtain specific range? (FAA-H-8083-25)

Specific range can be defined in the following relationship:

a. NM divided by pounds of fuel, *or*

b. NM per hour divided by pounds of fuel per hour, *or*

c. Knots divided by fuel flow.

3. How would a maximum range condition be achieved?
(FAA-H-8083-25)

The maximum range condition is obtained at maximum lift/drag ratio (L/D_{MAX}). It is important to note that for a given configuration, the L/D_{MAX} occurs at a particular AOA and lift coefficient and is unaffected by weight or altitude.

4. What is lift/drag ratio? (FAA-H-8083-25)

The lift-to-drag ratio is the efficiency of an airfoil section. It is the ratio of the coefficient of lift to the coefficient of drag for any given angle of attack.

5. A change in weight will alter which values required to obtain L/D_{MAX}? (FAA-H-8083-25)

A variation in weight will alter the values of airspeed and power necessary to obtain the L/D_{MAX}.

6. During cruise flight, what should a pilot do to maintain L/D_{MAX}? (FAA-H-8083-25)

Variations of speed and power required must be monitored as part of the cruise control procedure to maintain the L/D_{MAX}.

7. How would you obtain specific endurance?
(FAA-H-8083-25)

Specific endurance refers to flying time per pound of fuel burned and is determined by taking the flight time and dividing by fuel flow in pounds per hour. The ability of the airplane to convert fuel energy into flying time is an important factor in flying operations. The specific endurance of the airplane is defined as follows:

$$\text{specific endurance} = \frac{\text{flight hours}}{\text{pounds of fuel}}$$

8. How would a maximum endurance condition be achieved? (FAA-H-8083-25)

At the point of minimum power required, since this condition would require the lowest fuel flow to keep the airplane in steady level flight.

9. What engine inoperative enroute performance is required for turbine-powered transport category airplanes? (Order 8900.1)

These airplanes must, at all points along the intended route after an engine fails, be able to clear all terrain and obstructions by 1,000 feet that are within 5 statute miles on either side of the intended track. This requirement must be met at the forecast temperature for the required altitudes at the planned time of the flight.

10. Define the term "driftdown." (Order 8900.1)

A procedure by which an airplane, with one or more engines inoperative, the remaining engines at maximum continuous thrust (MCT) and while maintaining a specified speed (usually best L/D × 1.01%), descends to the altitude at which the airplane can maintain altitude and begin to climb (this altitude is defined as driftdown height).

11. What are several examples of performance charts used for enroute/cruise data?

a. High speed, intermediate and long range cruise power

b. One engine inoperative cruise power

c. Holding time

d. Endurance and range profile

12. In which altitude range is the minimum specific fuel consumption of a turboprop engine normally available? (FAA-H-8083-25)

25,000 feet to the tropopause (35,000 feet).

C. Descent and Landing

1. How will you calculate your distance to descend when planning for an IFR descent? (FAA-H-8083-6)

$$\frac{\text{cruising altitude} - \text{descent altitude}}{\text{descent rate (ft/min)}} \times \frac{\text{ground speed (NM/hr)}}{60 \text{ (min/hr)}}$$

= NM required

Example:

$$\frac{11,000 - 3,000 \text{ ft.}}{1,000 \text{ ft/min}} \times \frac{180 \text{ NM/hr}}{60 \text{ (min/hr)}}$$

$$= \frac{8,000 \text{ ft.}}{1,000 \text{ ft/min}} \times 3 \text{ NM/min}$$

$$= 8 \times 3 = 24 \text{ NM}$$

2. Define the following symbols. (14 CFR Part 1)

V_S — stalling speed or the minimum steady flight speed at which the airplane is controllable.
V_{S0} — stalling speed or the minimum steady flight speed in the landing configuration.
V_{S1} — stalling speed or minimum steady flight speed obtained in a specified configuration.

3. What is the definition of "V_{REF}"? (FAA-H-8083-3)

Reference landing speed — turbine aircraft operate at a number of different weights, requiring an adjustment to the airspeed for a given approach and landing. V_{REF} is calculated for each landing and is usually $1.3 \times V_{S0}$. Normally found on TOLD cards where V_{REF} has been calculated in advance for a variety of configuration/weight/temperature combinations.

4. Define the term "approach climb weight." (Order 8900.1)

Airplane weight during approach must be planned so that a specified gradient of climb is available with one engine inoperative, at takeoff thrust, and at the temperature forecasted to exist on arrival. The approach climb weight requirement is intended to guarantee adequate performance in the go-around configuration after an approach with an inoperative engine (gear up, flaps at the specified approach setting, the critical engine inoperative, and remaining engines at go-around thrust).

5. Define the term "landing climb weight." (Order 8900.1)

For release, the weight of the airplane (allowing for normal enroute fuel and oil consumption) must result in a landing approach weight at which the airplane can climb at a gradient of 3.2% or better. This requirement is intended to guarantee adequate performance to arrest the descent and allow a go-around from the final stage of a landing (gear down, landing flaps, and go-around thrust).

6. What landing distance limitations apply to turbine-powered aircraft? (Order 8900.1)

a. Turbojets must be able (allowing for normal enroute fuel and oil consumption) to land within 60% of the effective runway at both the destination and the alternate airports.

b. Turboprop airplanes must be able to land within 60% of the effective runway at the destination and 70% at the alternate airport.

c. A flight may be dispatched that cannot meet the 60% runway requirement at the destination, *if* an alternate airport is designated where the flight can land within the distance specified for an alternate airport.

d. When a runway is forecasted to be wet or slippery at the destination, 15% must be added to the required landing runway length. A correction is not applied to the alternate landing runway length for preflight planning.

7. What is the most efficient braking procedure for turboprop aircraft? (FAA-H-8083-3)

Reverse-thrust propellers should be applied as soon as possible after touchdown to reduce landing distance to a minimum. Braking should occur as the aircraft slows and wing lift is reduced.

8. **Define the term "hydroplaning."** (Order 8900.1)

   Hydroplaning occurs when the tires are lifted off a runway surface by the combination of aircraft speed and a thin film of water present on the runway.

9. **What are the three basic types of hydroplaning?**
   (Order 8900.1)

   Dynamic—occurs when there is standing water on the runway surface. Water about 1/10th of an inch deep acts to lift the tire off the runway. The minimum speed at which dynamic hydroplaning occurs has been determined to be 8.6 times the square root of the tire pressure in pounds per square inch.

   Viscous—occurs as a result of the viscous properties of water. A very thin film of fluid cannot be penetrated by the tire and the tire consequently rolls on top of the film. Viscous hydroplaning can occur at much slower speeds than dynamic hydroplaning but requires a smooth acting surface.

   Reverted Rubber Hydroplaning—occurs when a pilot, during the landing roll, locks the brakes for an extended period of time while on a wet runway. The friction creates heat, which combined with water creates a steam layer between the aircraft tire and runway surface.

10. **What is the best method of speed reduction if hydroplaning is experienced on landing?**
    (Order 8900.1, FAA-H-8083-3)

    Aerodynamic braking is the most effective means of dealing with a hydroplaning situation. Use of flaps, increased angle of attack, spoilers, reverse thrust, etc., will produce more desirable results than braking.

11. **What effect does landing at high elevation airports have on ground speed with comparable conditions relative to temperature, wind, and airplane weight?** (FAA-H-8083-3)

    Indicated airspeed will remain the same, but the ground speed will be higher due to reduced air density.

12. **What is the recommended terminology for describing braking action?** (AIM 4-3-8)

    When available, ATC furnishes pilots the quality of braking action received from pilots or airport management. The quality of braking action is described by the terms "good," "fair," "poor," and "nil," or a combination of these terms. When pilots report the quality of braking action by using the terms noted above, they should use descriptive terms that are easily understood, such as, "braking action poor the first/last half of the runway," together with the particular type of aircraft.

13. **What are several examples of performance charts used for descent and landing data?**

    a. Time, fuel, and distance to descend

    b. Maximum landing weight

    c. Climb—balked landing

    d. Normal landing distance

    e. Landing distance—one engine inoperative

D. Limitations

1. **Define the following airspeed limitations.** (FAA-H-8083-25)

    V_A—maneuvering speed. The design maneuvering airspeed, which is the maximum speed at which the limit load can be imposed (either by gusts or full deflection of the control surfaces) without causing structural damage.

    V_B—design speed for maximum gust intensity. Also known as turbulent air penetration speed.

    V_{FE}—maximum flap extended speed. The highest airspeed permissible with the wing flaps in a prescribed extended position. This is a problem involving the airloads imposed on the structure of the flaps.

    Continued

V_{LO}—maximum landing gear operating speed. The maximum airspeed at which the landing gear can be safely extended or retracted. This is a problem involving the airloads imposed on the operating mechanism during extension or retraction of the gear.

V_{LE}—maximum landing gear extended speed. It is the maximum airspeed at which the airplane can be safely flown with the landing gear extended, which is a problem involving stability and controllability.

V_{MC}—the airspeed at which, when the critical engine is suddenly made inoperative, it is possible to maintain control of the airplane with that engine still inoperative and maintain straight flight with a bank angle of not more than 5 degrees.

V_{MO}—velocity maximum operation is an airplane's indicated airspeed limit. Exceeding V_{MO} may cause aerodynamic flutter and G-load limitations to become critical during the dive recovery.

2. What is the significance of the red and white hash-marked pointer on the airspeed indicator? (FAA-H-8083-3)

This pointer indicates the maximum operating speed for any operation. It is self-adjusting with changes in altitude.

3. What limitations apply to engine operation?

Several limitations should be observed when operating a turbine engine. Exceeding any of these usually requires a maintenance inspection before further operation. Limitations should be observed in each of the different phases of aircraft operation, such as starting, idle, takeoff, maximum continuous power, cruise climb and cruise, maximum reverse, etc.; some examples are:

a. Maximum torque

b. Maximum observed ITT (T6)

c. Maximum and minimum N1 and N2 (low and high speed compressor speed)

d. Maximum and minimum Np (prop RPM)

e. Maximum and minimum oil pressure

f. Maximum and minimum oil temperature

4. What are several examples of limitations that apply when starting?

a. *External power limits*—the external power source (GPU) should be capable of generating sufficient volts and amps for starting.

b. *Starter limits*—use of the starter is limited in the amount of time it may be continuously operated. Exceeding these times will usually result in overheating and damage to the starter's internal components. (Example: 30 seconds ON, 3 minutes OFF, 30 seconds ON, 3 minutes OFF, 30 seconds ON, 30 minutes OFF.)

5. What limitations apply to aircraft generators?

a. Maximum sustained generator load limits apply for a specified minimum N1 value.

b. Minimum N1 values are specified for a given generator load.

6. Are there any limitations concerning outside air temperatures?

Yes—minimum and maximum outside air temperature limits must be observed. Minimum outside air temperatures affect oil temperature for fuel heater operation. A minimum fuel temperature must be maintained to avoid fuel system icing. Maximum outside air temperatures have limitations due to their effect on engine operational temperature limits. Also, maximum temperatures are sometimes specified for avionics in the cockpit.

7. Are there any limitations that apply to the aircraft fuel system?

Yes—examples of these are:

a. Use only the recommended fuels, normally Jet A, Jet A-1, Jet B, etc.

b. In the event recommended fuel is not available, only certain fuels may be used (i.e. 80, 80/87, 91/96, 100, 100LL, etc.).

Continued

c. Limitations to use of emergency engine fuels; such as length of time they can be used between engine overhauls, maximum altitude limitations, inoperative equipment limitations (i.e., auxiliary pumps must be operational).

d. Maximum allowable fuel imbalance between wing fuel tanks.

e. Minimum fuel quantities in auxiliary and main tanks.

f. Minimum fuel system pressures.

8. What is one major limitation that applies to the cabin pressurization system? (AC 65-15A)

Maximum cabin differential pressure — if the differential pressure becomes too great, structural damage to the fuselage may occur. Depending on the particular aircraft, maximum cabin differential pressure values will vary. The design, manufacturing, and selection of structural materials, as well as engine bleed-air capacity (which maintains a constant volume of airflow to the fuselage) all affect it.

9. State the different weight limitations that apply when conducting large aircraft operations. (FAA-H-8083-1)

a. Maximum ramp weight

b. Maximum takeoff weight

c. Maximum landing weight

d. Maximum zero fuel weight

e. Maximum weight in the cargo compartments

f. Cabin floor loading

10. What limitations apply concerning the types of maneuvers an aircraft is approved for? (FAA-H-8083-25)

The category the aircraft was certified under determines the type of maneuvers it is approved for. Normal category aircraft are prohibited from acrobatic maneuvers including spins.

11. What limitations apply concerning load factor on an aircraft? (FAA-H-8083-25)

Flight load factor limits are specified for all aircraft. Limiting load factors are given for both "flaps up" and "flaps down" configurations. If these limitations are exceeded, the aircraft is usually taken out of service and inspected by maintenance before being allowed to return to service.

12. What are some examples of limitations that apply to the propeller?

a. Propeller rotational speed limits (transient, reverse).

b. Propeller rotational overspeed limits (max rpm, time limits).

E. Multi-Engine Powerplant Failure

1. Define the term "critical engine." (14 CFR Part 1)

The "critical" engine is that engine whose failure would most adversely affect the performance or handling qualities of the airplane.

2. On most multi-engine aircraft, what engine is normally considered the critical engine? (FAA-H-8083-3)

This is the left engine, because its failure requires the most rudder force to overcome yaw.

3. Discuss the effects of P-factor in a multi-engine airplane. (FAA-H-8083-3)

In most multi-engine aircraft, both engines rotate to the right (clockwise) when viewed from the rear, and both engines develop an equal amount of thrust. At low airspeed and high power conditions, the downward moving propeller blade of each engine develops more thrust than the upward moving blade. This asymmetric propeller thrust or "P-factor" results in a center of thrust at the right side of each engine.

The turning (or yawing) force of the right engine is greater than the left engine because the center of thrust is much farther away from the center line of the fuselage—it has a longer level arm. Thus, when the right engine is operative and the left engine is inoperative, the turning or yawing force is greater than the opposite situation of an operative left and an inoperative right engine. In other words, directional control may be difficult when the left engine (the critical engine) is suddenly made inoperative.

4. Why does a multi-engine airplane with one engine inoperative roll in the direction of the inoperative engine? (FAA-P-8740-19)

Loss of power on one engine reduces the induced airflow from the propeller slipstream over that wing. As a result, total lift for that wing is substantially reduced, causing the airplane to roll in the direction of the inoperative engine. Yaw also affects the lift distribution over the wing, further contributing to this roll. These roll forces may be balanced by banking into the operative engine as well as application of rudder opposite to the direction of yaw.

5. Why does a multi-engine airplane become directionally uncontrollable during flight at an airspeed less than V_{MC}? (FAA-H-8083-3)

When one engine fails, the pilot must overcome the asymmetrical thrust (except on airplanes with centerline thrust) created by the operating engine by setting up a counteracting moment with the rudder. When the rudder is fully deflected, its yawing power will depend upon the velocity of airflow across the rudder, which in turn is dependent upon the airspeed. As the airplane decelerates, it will reach a speed below which the rudder moment will no longer balance the thrust moment and directional control will be lost.

6. Why is flight below V_{MC} so dangerous? (FAA-H-8083-3)

With full power applied to the operating engine, as the airspeed drops below V_{MC} the airplane tends to roll as well as yaw into the inoperative engine. This tendency becomes greater as the airspeed is further reduced; since this tendency must be counteracted by aileron control, the yaw condition is aggravated further by aileron yaw (adverse yaw). If a stall should occur in this condition (highly likely), a violent roll into the dead engine may be experienced. Such an event near the ground could be disastrous.

7. Explain why the movement of the center of gravity (CG) affects V_{MC}. (FAA-H-8083-3)

V_{MC} is greater when the CG is at the rearmost allowable position. Since the airplane rotates around the center of gravity, the moments are measured using that point as a reference. A rearward CG would not affect a thrust moment, but would shorten the arm to the center of the rudder's horizontal lift which would mean a higher force (airspeed) would be required to counteract the engine-out yaw.

8. Explain how a sideslip condition affects V_{MC}. (FAA-H-8083-3)

During engine-out flight, the large rudder deflection required to counteract the asymmetric thrust also results in a "lateral lift" force on the vertical fin. The lateral lift represents an unbalanced side force on the airplane that is counteracted by allowing the airplane to accelerate sideways until the lateral drag caused by the sideslip equals the rudder lift force. The wings will be level, the ball in the turn-and-slip indicator will be centered and the airplane will be in a moderate sideslip toward the inoperative engine. A "sideslip" condition will result in the following:

a. The relative wind blowing on the inoperative engine side of the vertical fin tends to increase the asymmetric moment caused by the failure of one engine.

b. The resulting sideslip severely degrades stall characteristics.

c. The additional rudder deflection required to balance the extra moment and the sideslip drag causes a significant reduction in climb and/or acceleration capability.

d. V_{MC} will be higher.

9. Why is it necessary to bank toward the operative engine in an engine-out emergency? (FAA-H-8083-3)

If the wings are kept level and the ball in the turn coordinator centered, the airplane will be in a moderate sideslip toward the inoperative engine resulting in a substantial increase in V_{MC}, and a significant reduction in climb and/or acceleration capability. By establishing a bank toward the operative engine, a component of the aircraft's weight is utilized to counteract the rudder-induced sideforce present in the sideslip. At a specific angle of bank, the airplane will be in a zero-sideslip condition, which will result in adequate directional control as well as a substantial increase in engine-out performance (rate of climb). Decreasing the bank angle away from the operative engine increases V_{MC} at the rate of approximately 3 knots per degree of bank.

Continued

Note: Banking into the operative engine, beyond that necessary for a zero sideslip condition, may increase rudder authority and assist in directional control initially but it will also DRASTICALLY reduce the airplane's climb performance. Once directional control has been achieved, a reduction in bank angle, as necessary to achieve a zero-sideslip condition, must be established in order to obtain the necessary climb performance.

F. High Speed Flight

1. Define the term MACH number. (AC 61-107)

MACH number is a decimal number (M) representing the true airspeed (TAS) relationship to the local speed of sound (e.g., TAS 75 percent (0.75 M) of the speed of sound, where 100 percent of the speed of sound is represented as MACH 1 (1.0 M)). The local speed of sound varies with changes in temperature.

2. Define the term critical MACH number. (AC 61-107)

The critical MACH number is the free stream MACH number at which local sonic flow such as buffet, airflow separation, and shock waves become evident. These phenomena occur above the critical MACH number, often referred to as MACH crit. These phenomena are listed as follows:

Subsonic — MACH Numbers below 0.75

Transonic — MACH Numbers from 0.75 to 1.20

Supersonic — MACH Numbers from 1.20 to 5.0

Hypersonic — MACH Numbers above 5.0

3. Define MACH speed. (AC 61-107)

MACH speed is the ratio of the aircraft's true airspeed to the local speed of sound. At sea level, on a standard day (59°F/15°C) the speed of sound equals approximately 660 kts or 1,120 feet per second. MACH 0.75 at sea level is equivalent to a TAS of approximately 498 kts (0.75 × 660 kts) or 840 feet per second. The temperature of the atmosphere normally decreases with an increase in altitude, and the speed of sound is directly related only to temperature. The result is a decrease in the speed of sound up to about 36,000 feet.

4. What is MACH "tuck" and why does it occur? (AC 61-107)

MACH "tuck" is the result of an aftward shift in the center of lift causing a nose-down pitching moment. MACH tuck is caused principally by two basic factors:

a. Shockwave-induced flow separation, which normally begins near the wing root, causes a decrease in the downwash velocity over the elevator and produces a tendency for the aircraft to nose down.

b. Aftward movement of the center of pressure, which tends to unbalance the equilibrium of the aircraft in relation to its center of gravity (CG) in subsonic flight.

5. What is MACH buffet? (AC 61-107)

MACH buffet is the airflow separation behind a shockwave pressure barrier caused by airflow over flight surfaces exceeding the speed of sound.

6. What are MACH trim compensators? (AC 61-107)

Because of the critical aspects of high altitude/high MACH flight, most turbojet airplanes capable of operating in the MACH speed ranges are designed with some form of trim and autopilot MACH compensating device (also known as a "stick puller") to alert the pilot to inadvertent excursions beyond its certificated M_{MO}.

7. Define the symbol M_{MO}. (AC 61-107)

M_{MO} — MACH maximum operation. This is the airplane's maximum certificated MACH number. Any excursion past M_{MO}, whether intentional or accidental, may cause induced flow separation of boundary layer air over the ailerons and elevators of an airplane. This results in a loss of control surface authority and/or control surface buzz or snatch.

8. What is Q-Corner or Coffin Corner? (AC 61-107)

Coffin corner is a term used to describe operations at high altitudes where low indicated airspeeds yield high true airspeeds (MACH number) at high angles of attack. The high angle of attack results in flow separation, which causes buffet. Turning maneuvers at these altitudes increase the angle of attack and result in stability

deterioration with a decrease in control effectiveness. The relationship of stall speed to MACH crit narrows to a point where sudden
increases in angle of attack, roll rates, and/or disturbances; e.g.,
clear air turbulence, cause the limits of the airspeed envelope to be
exceeded. Coffin corner exists in the upper portion of the maneuvering envelope for a given gross weight and G-force.

9. What is a "Dutch roll"? (AC 61-107)

A "Dutch roll" is a coupled oscillation in roll and yaw that
becomes objectionable when roll, or lateral stability is reduced in
comparison with yaw or directional stability. A stability augmentation system is required to be installed on the aircraft to dampen
the Dutch roll tendency when it is determined to be objectionable,
or when it adversely affects the control stability requirements
for certification. The yaw damper is a gyro-operated autocontrol
system installed to provide rudder input and aid in canceling out
yaw tendencies such as those in Dutch roll.

10. What is adverse yaw? (AC 61-107)

A phenomenon in which the airplane heading changes in a direction opposite to that commanded by a roll control input. It is the
result of unequal lift and drag characteristics of the down-going
and up-going wings. The phenomena are alleviated by tailoring the
control design through use of spoilers, yaw dampers, and interconnected rudder and aileron systems.

G. Weight and Balance

1. Define the following weights. (FAA-H-8083-1)

Empty weight—the weight of the airframe, engines, all perma-
nently installed equipment, and unusable fuel. Depending upon the
part of the federal regulations under which the aircraft was certificated, either the undrainable oil or full reservoir of oil is included.

Basic operating weight (BOW)—the empty weight of the aircraft
plus the weight of the required crew, their baggage and other standard item such as meals and potable water.

Maximum zero fuel weight—the maximum authorized weight of an aircraft without fuel. This is the total weight for a particular flight less the fuel. It includes the aircraft and everything that will be carried on the flight except the weight of the fuel.

Maximum ramp weight—the maximum weight approved for ground maneuver. It includes weight of start, taxi, and runup fuel.

Maximum takeoff weight—the maximum weight approved for the start of the takeoff run.

Maximum landing weight—the maximum weight approved for the landing touchdown.

2. What is the definition of MAC? (FAA-H-8083-1)

Mean aerodynamic chord is the chord of an imaginary airfoil that has all of the aerodynamic characteristics of the actual airfoil. It can be thought of as the chord drawn through the geographic center of the plan area of the wing.

3. Explain the term "percent of mean aerodynamic chord." (FAA-H-8083-1)

Expression of the CG relative to the MAC is a common practice in larger aircraft. The CG position is expressed as a percent MAC (percent of mean aerodynamic chord) and the CG limits are expressed in the same manner. Normally, an aircraft will have acceptable flight characteristics if the CG is located somewhere near the 25% average chord point. This means the CG is located one-fourth of the total distance back from the leading edge of the average wing section.

4. What is the definition of LEMAC and TEMAC? (FAA-H-8083-1)

LEMAC—leading edge of the mean aerodynamic chord expressed in inches aft of the datum.

TEMAC—trailing edge of the mean aerodynamic chord expressed in inches aft of the datum.

5. What is the formula for determining percent MAC? (FAA-H-8083-1)

$$\text{CG in \%MAC} = \frac{\text{CG in inches from LEMAC} \times 100}{\text{MAC}}$$

Example:
The loaded CG is 42.47 inches aft of the datum.
The MAC is 61.6 inches long.
The LEMAC is located at station 20.1.
The CG is 42.47 – 20.1 = 22.37 inches aft of LEMAC.
The loaded CG is located at 36.3% of the mean aerodynamic chord.

6. What are the standard weights assumed for the following when calculating weight and balance problems? (AC 120-27C)

Adult Passenger .... 190 lbs (summer); 195 lbs (winter)*
Male .... 200 lbs (summer); 205 lbs (winter)*
Female................................... 179 lbs (summer); 184 lbs (winter)*
Children .... 82 lbs (summer); 87 lbs (winter)*
Fuel .... 6.0 lbs/U.S. gal
Jet Fuel................................. 6.7 lbs/U.S. gal
Oil .... 7.5 lbs/U.S. gal
Water..................................... 8.35 lbs/U.S. gal

Note: Summer—May 1 through October 31
           Winter—November 1 through April 30

7. Describe a typical weight and balance calculation for a turboprop aircraft.

Weight: Takeoff weight is checked against the maximum allowable takeoff weight for the particular flight, which is usually obtained from airport analysis charts and cannot be exceeded. Landing weight is also checked against the maximum allowable landing weight for the destination, ensuring that it has not been exceeded.

a. Basic operating weight + Adult weight + Child weight + Cargo weight = Zero fuel weight

b. Zero fuel weight + Fuel on board weight = Ramp weight

c. Ramp weight – Ground fuel weight = Takeoff weight

d. Takeoff weight – Enroute fuel weight = Landing weight

Balance: Most commuter airlines use a variety of methods to make balance computations quickly, such as quick reference charts, slide-rule-type computers, loading summary charts, etc. The approved random loading rules that establish minimum/maximum amounts of weight in each of the aircraft compartments also provide the ground/flight crew with a quick and efficient method of loading the aircraft within CG.

8. How can a pilot determine cargo pallet loads are within floor loading limits? (FAA-H-8083-1)

Each cargo hold has a structural floor-loading limit based on the weight of the load and the area over which this weight is distributed. To determine the maximum weight of a loaded cargo pallet that can be carried in a cargo hold, divide its total weight, which includes the weight of the empty pallet and its tie-down devices, by its area in square feet. This load per square foot must be equal to or less than the floor load limit.

9. Determine the maximum load that can be placed on this pallet without exceeding the floor load limit. (FAA-H-8083-1)

Pallet dimensions: 36×48 in
Empty pallet weight: 47 lbs
Tie-down devices: 33 lbs
Floor load limit: 169 lbs per square foot
Floor Load—Caution

The pallet has an area of 36 inches (3 feet) by 48 inches (4 feet). This is equal to 12 square feet. The floor has a load limit of 169 lbs per square foot; therefore, the total weight of the loaded pallet can be $169 \times 12 = 2,028$ lbs. Subtracting the weight of the pallet and the tie-down devices gives an allowable load of 1,948 lbs.

$(2,028 - [47 + 33])$

10. What is a "load manifest"?

A "load manifest" is usually a simple, standardized form that provides a pilot with a positive, accurate and efficient means of calculating and recording the weight and balance condition of the aircraft before each flight.

11. What type of information is required on a load manifest? (Order 8900.1)

A domestic operator must prepare a load manifest containing the following:

a. Weight of the aircraft, fuel and oil, cargo, baggage, passengers, and crewmembers.

b. Maximum allowable weight at which the flight can comply with the requirements of 14 CFR Part 121.

c. Actual weight at takeoff.

d. Evidence that the aircraft is loaded within weight and balance limitations.

e. Passenger names (unless this information is maintained by other means).

12. What is a load manifest worksheet?

Ground personnel responsible for loading an aircraft use this document. As cargo and passengers are loaded, the load manifest worksheet is updated; when aircraft loading is complete, it is signed and forwarded to the flight crew. It provides accurate passenger and cargo load information to the flight crew for final weight and balance calculations.

13. Define the following terms.

Carry-on bags—bags allowed to be carried on board by a passenger. Stowed in overhead bins or under a seat; usually one carry-on bag per passenger.

Checked bags—bags checked in at the ticket counter or gate and not carried on by the passenger. Loaded by ramp personnel and reclaimed by the passenger at baggage claim.

COMAT—company material. This is non-revenue company material such as inter-departmental correspondence, payroll, and miscellaneous items. All COMAT must be weighed and noted on the load manifest worksheet.

HAZMAT—hazardous material. 49 CFR governs the acceptance, handling and carriage of dangerous goods by all forms of transportation including the airlines. The airline must provide required training and procedures to all appropriate personnel.

14. What is meant by the term "maxed out" with reference to aircraft weight and balance?

This term is used when the aircraft is loaded with the maximum number of passengers and bags/cargo.

15. What are some of the problems caused by overloading an aircraft? (FAA-H-8083-1)

a. The aircraft will need a higher takeoff speed, which results in a longer takeoff run.

b. Both the rate and angle of climb will be reduced.

c. The service ceiling will be lowered.

d. The cruising speed will be reduced.

e. The cruising range will be shortened.

f. Maneuverability will be decreased.

g. A longer landing roll will be required because the landing speed will be higher.

h. Excessive loads will be imposed on the structure, especially the landing gear.

16. State some factors that may cause the CG to move while in flight.

a. Movement of passengers and flight attendants from their normal seat position in the aircraft cabin.

b. Landing gear retraction.

c. Fuel burn and movement of fuel in large aircraft.

17. What effect does a forward center of gravity have on an aircraft's flight characteristics? (FAA-H-8083-25)

Higher stall speed—stalling angle of attack reached at a higher speed due to increased wing loading.

Slower cruise speed—increased drag, greater angle of attack required to maintain altitude.

More stable—when angle of attack increased, the airplane tends to reduce angle of attack; longitudinal stability.

Greater back elevator pressure required—longer takeoff roll, higher approach speeds and problems with the landing flare.

18. **What effect does an aft center of gravity have on an aircraft's flight characteristics?** (FAA-H-8083-25)

Lower stall speed—less wing loading.

Higher cruise speed—reduced drag, smaller angle of attack required to maintain altitude.

Less stable—stall and spin recovery more difficult. When angle of attack is increased it tends to result in even more increased angle of attack.

Operational
Procedures

3

A. Certificates and Documents

1. What types of certificates and documents are found on board transport category aircraft? (Order 8900.1)

a. Aircraft Flight Manual (AFM)

b. Airworthiness certificate

c. Registration certificate

d. Radio station license

e. Airport runway analysis

f. Minimum Equipment List (MEL)

g. Maintenance records

h. Supplemental performance manual

i. Operations manual

j. Takeoff and Landing Data Cards (TOLD)

k. Quick reference handbook (normal, abnormal and emergency checklists)

2. What are Operations Specifications? (14 CFR §119.5)

The Operations Specifications for a Part 121 or 135 operator authorize the certificate holder to operate in a certain geographic area; also contains other specifications such as maintenance procedures, emergency procedures, etc. Provide the guidelines an airline must adhere to when conducting normal operations.

3. What is a Minimum Equipment List (MEL)? (Order 8900.1)

The FAA has found that for particular situations, an acceptable level of safety can be maintained with specific items of equipment inoperative for a limited period of time, until repairs can be made. The MEL describes the limitations that apply when an operator wishes to conduct operations under these circumstances—it takes into consideration the operator's particular aircraft configuration, operational procedures and conditions. The regulations require that the MEL be carried aboard the aircraft or that the flightcrew have direct access to the MEL information prior to flight.

4. What is a Configuration Deviation List (CDL)?
(Order 8900.1)

Aircraft certified under the provisions of CAR, 14 CFR Parts 23 or 25, and intended for use under 14 CFR Parts 121 or 135 may be approved for operations with missing secondary airframe and engine parts; the source document for such operations is the CDL. The Aircraft Certification Office grants approval of the CDL under an amendment to the type certificate. For U.S.-certificated aircraft, the CDL is incorporated into the limitations section of the AFM as an appendix.

5. What is meant by the term "deferred maintenance"?
(Order 8900.1)

The operator's approved MEL allows the operator to continue a flight or series of flights with certain inoperative equipment. The continued operation must meet the requirements of the MEL deferral classification and the requirements for the equipment loss.

6. What is the purpose of a company flight operations manual (CFM)? (Order 8900.1)

A company flight operations manual (CFM) provides information on policy, procedures and guidance in such areas as flight crew responsibilities, normal/abnormal procedures, emergency procedures, limitations, etc. The CFM is essentially an AFM (aircraft flight manual) specifically tailored to the operator's particular operation. The regulations require that a flight manual be available in the aircraft for flightcrew use and guidance during flight operations.

B. Dispatch

1. What is an aircraft dispatcher's function?

An aircraft dispatcher is an FAA-certificated individual who exercises responsibility, along with the pilot-in-command, in the operational control of a flight. Domestic and flag operators must use certified aircraft dispatchers to directly control flight operations. A pilot-in-command may not initiate or continue a flight unless both the PIC and the aircraft dispatcher agree that the flight can be conducted safely as planned under the existing and forecast conditions. Once a flight is initiated, the aircraft dispatcher must continually monitor the flight's progress and inform the PIC of conditions that could affect the safe operation of that flight.

2. Define the term "operational control." (14 CFR Part 1)

Operational control, with respect to a flight, means the exercise of authority over initiating, conducting or terminating a flight.

3. What are the responsibilities of an aircraft dispatcher? (Order 8900.1)

These include:

a. Weight and balance computations and load control procedures.

b. Aircraft performance computations, including takeoff weight limitations based on departure runway, arrival runway, and enroute limitations, and also engine-out limitations.

c. Flight planning procedures, including route selection, flight time, and fuel requirements analysis.

d. Dispatch release preparation.

e. Crew briefings (weather, NOTAMs, etc.).

f. Flight monitoring procedures.

g. MEL and CDL procedures.

h. ATC and instrument procedures, including ground hold and central flow control procedures.

i. Emergency procedures.

4. What is a dispatch release? (Order 8900.1)

A flight conducted under Part 121 domestic or flag rules may not depart from the point of origin unless a dispatch release contains specific authorization for the flight between specified points. The dispatch release may be for a single flight or for a series of flights with intermediate stops.

5. What information is required to be included in all dispatch releases? (Order 8900.1)

Dispatch releases must contain at least the following information:

a. Aircraft identification number

b. Flight number

c. Departure airport, intermediate stops, destination airports, and alternate airports

d. Type of operation (IFR or VFR)

e. Minimum fuel quantity required

f. Current weather information

6. How does the flight crew determine how much fuel should be added for a particular flight?

A flight dispatcher responsible for the flight determines the amount of fuel necessary, considering regulatory requirements, weather, and projected passenger/cargo loads. The captain reviews the flight release prepared by the dispatcher which indicates proposed routing, alternates, fuel burn, required fuel, etc. If in agreement, the aircraft is fueled accordingly. If not, the captain notifies the dispatcher and a mutual agreement is eventually achieved.

C. Preflight

1. Give examples of preflight activities that airline flightcrews are responsible for. (Order 8900.1)

a. Flight planning activities, such as review of weather, flight plans, anticipated takeoff weight and performance data, flight control requirements (dispatch, flight release, flight locating, ATC flight plans).

b. Aircraft preflight activities, such as exterior walkaround, aircraft logbook reviews, and cockpit setup procedures, including stowage of flightcrew baggage and professional equipment.

c. Flight attendant inspection of cabin emergency equipment and cabin setup procedures, including stowage of flight attendant baggage and professional equipment.

2. **What are some examples of professional equipment that flight crewmembers are responsible for and should be in possession of when preparing for a flight?** (Order 8900.1)

These include aeronautical charts, appropriate operator manuals, and operable flashlights. All charts and manuals carried by crewmembers should be current.

3. **What types of placards are required in transport category aircraft?** (Order 8900.1)

Required placards and signs include seatbelt and flotation equipment placards at seats; emergency/safety equipment placards; weight restriction placards; no smoking/seatbelt signs; no smoking placards; exit signs and placards including door opening instructions.

D. Fueling

1. **What type of fuel is used in turbine engine powered aircraft?** (FAA-H-8083-30)

The aircraft gas turbine is designed to operate on a distillate fuel, commonly called jet fuel. Jet fuels are also composed of hydrocarbons with a little more carbon and usually a higher sulfur content than gasoline. Inhibitors may be added to reduce corrosion and oxidation. Anti-icing additives are also blended to prevent fuel icing.

2. **What are the two main types of jet fuel in common use today?** (FAA-H-8083-30)

Jet A—a kerosene grade turbine fuel

Jet B—a blend of gasoline and kerosene fractions

Note: There is also a third type, called Jet A-1, which is made for operation in extremely low temperatures.

3. What is the difference between Jet A and Jet B fuel? (FAA-H-8083-30)

There is very little physical difference between Jet A (JP-5) fuel and commercial kerosene. Jet A was developed as a heavy kerosene having a higher flash point and lower freezing point than most kerosenes. It has a very low vapor pressure, so there is little loss of fuel from evaporation or boil-off at higher altitudes. It contains more heat energy per gallon than does Jet B (JP-4).

Jet B is similar to Jet A. It is a blend of gasoline and kerosene fractions. Most commercial turbine engines will operate on either Jet A or Jet B fuel. However, the difference in the specific gravity of the fuels may require fuel control adjustments. Therefore, the fuels cannot always be considered interchangeable.

4. Why are jet fuels more susceptible to water contamination than aviation gasoline? (FAA-H-8083-30)

Both Jet A and Jet B fuels are blends of heavy distillates and tend to absorb water. The specific gravity of jet fuels, especially kerosene, is closer to water than is aviation gasoline; thus, any water introduced into the fuel, either through refueling or condensation, will take an appreciable time to settle out. At high altitudes where low temperatures are encountered, water droplets combine with the fuel to form a frozen substance referred to as "gel." The mass of "gel" or "icing" that may be generated from moisture held in suspension in jet fuel can be much greater than in gasoline.

5. When ordering additional fuel for turbine aircraft, what formula may be used to convert pounds of fuel to gallons?

Take the fuel to be added in pounds and divide by 10; multiply this value by 1.5; the result equals fuel to be added in gallons.

6. What is the purpose of jettisoning fuel? (FAA-H-8083-1)

Most large aircraft are approved for a greater weight for takeoff than for landing. Pilots have the ability to jettison (dump) fuel out of the aircraft in the event that an emergency landing is required soon after takeoff. The jettison system in most aircraft is designed so not all the fuel can be dumped—only enough to obtain a weight lower than maximum landing weight.

E. Safety of Flight

1. Discuss the positive exchange of flight controls concept. (FAA-H-8083-9)

Incident/accident statistics indicate a need to place additional emphasis on the exchange of control of an aircraft by pilots. Numerous accidents have occurred due to a lack of communication or misunderstanding as to who actually had control of the aircraft. A positive three-step process in the exchange of flight controls between pilots is a proven procedure and one that is strongly recommended. When one pilot wishes the other pilot to take control of the aircraft, he or she will say, "You have the flight controls." The other pilot acknowledges immediately by saying, "I have the flight controls." The first pilot again says, "You have the flight controls." When control is returned, follow the same procedure. A visual check is recommended to verify that the exchange has occurred. There should never be any doubt as to who is flying the aircraft.

2. Where are wake turbulence and wingtip vortices likely to occur? (AIM 7-3-3)

All aircraft generate turbulence and associated wingtip vortices. In general, avoid the area behind and below the generating aircraft, especially at low altitudes. Also of concern are the weight, speed, and shape of the wing of the generating aircraft. The greatest vortex strength occurs when the generating aircraft is *heavy, clean,* and *slow.*

3. What procedures should be followed to avoid wake turbulence when landing? (AIM 7-3-6)

a. *Landing behind a larger aircraft, on the same runway:* Stay at or above the larger aircraft's final approach flight path. Note its touchdown point and land beyond it.

b. *Landing behind a larger aircraft, on a parallel runway closer than 2,500 feet:* Consider possible drift to your runway. Stay at or above the larger aircraft's final approach flight path and note its touchdown point.

Continued

   c. *Landing behind a larger aircraft on a crossing runway:* Cross above the larger aircraft's flight path.

   d. *Landing behind a departing larger aircraft on the same runway:* Note the larger aircraft's rotation point, and land well prior to the rotation point.

   e. *Landing behind a departing larger aircraft on a crossing runway:* Note the larger aircraft's rotation point. If it is past the intersection, continue the approach, and land prior to the intersection. If the larger aircraft rotates prior to the intersection, avoid flight below the larger aircraft's flight path. Abandon the approach unless a landing is ensured well before you reach the intersection.

4. What procedures should be followed to avoid wake turbulence when taking off? (AIM 7-3-6)

   a. *Departing behind a larger aircraft:* Note the larger aircraft's rotation point, rotate prior to larger aircraft's rotation point. Continue climb above the larger aircraft's climb path until you turn clear of its wake.

   b. *Intersection takeoffs on the same runway:* Be alert to adjacent larger aircraft operations, particularly upwind of your runway. If you receive intersection takeoff clearance, avoid a subsequent heading that will cross below the larger aircraft's path.

   c. *Departing or landing after a larger aircraft executing a low approach, missed approach or touch-and-go landing:* Ensure that an interval of at least 2 minutes has elapsed before you take off or land. Because vortices settle and move laterally near the ground, the vortex hazard may continue to exist along the runway, particularly in light quartering wind situations.

   d. *Enroute VFR (thousand foot altitude plus 500 feet):* Avoid flight below and behind a large aircraft's path. If a larger aircraft is observed above on the same track (meeting or overtaking), adjust your position laterally, preferably upwind.

5. What wind condition prolongs the hazards of wake turbulence on a landing runway for the longest period of time? (AIM 7-3-4)

A crosswind will decrease the lateral movement of the wind vortex and increase the movement of the downwind vortex. Therefore a light wind with a cross-runway component of 1 to 5 knots could result in the upwind vortex remaining in the touchdown zone for a period of time, as well as hasten the drift of the downwind vortex toward another runway. Similarly, a tailwind condition can move the vortices of the preceding aircraft forward into the touchdown zone. The light quartering tailwind requires maximum caution.

6. For the purposes of wake turbulence separation, what are the various ATC aircraft classes? (P/CG)

a. *Heavy*—aircraft capable of takeoff weights of more than 255,000 pounds whether or not they are operating at this weight during a particular phase of flight.

b. *Large*—aircraft of more than 41,000 pounds, maximum certificated takeoff weight, up to 255,000 pounds.

c. *Small*—aircraft of 41,000 pounds or less maximum certificated takeoff weight.

7. What air traffic wake turbulence separations are provided in the following situations? (AIM 7-3-9)

a. Separation is applied to aircraft operating directly behind a heavy/B757 jet at the same altitude or less than 1,000 feet below:

    i. Heavy jet behind heavy jet—4 miles.

    ii. Large/heavy behind B757—4 miles.

    iii. Small behind B757—5 miles.

    iv. Small/large aircraft behind heavy jet—5 miles.

b. Separation measured at the time the preceding aircraft is over the landing threshold is provided to small aircraft:

    i. Small aircraft landing behind heavy jet—6 miles.

    ii. Small aircraft landing behind B757—5 miles.

    iii. Small aircraft landing behind large aircraft—4 miles.

8. **The acronym "LAHSO" refers to what specific air traffic control procedure?** (AIM 4-3-11)

   LAHSO ("Land and hold short operations"): At controlled airports, ATC may clear a pilot to land and hold short of an intersecting runway, an intersecting taxiway, or some other designated point on a runway other than an intersecting runway or taxiway. Pilots may accept such a clearance provided the pilot-in-command determines that the aircraft can safely land and stop within the available landing distance (ALD). Student pilots or pilots not familiar with LAHSO should not participate in the program.

9. **Where can available landing distance (ALD) data be found?** (AIM 4-3-11)

   ALD data are published in the special notices section of the A/FD, and in the U.S. Terminal Procedures Publications. Controllers will also provide ALD data upon request.

10. **Before accepting a LAHSO clearance, what information must a pilot have readily available?** (AIM 4-3-11)

    To conduct LAHSO, pilots should become familiar with all available information concerning LAHSO at their destination airport, and have readily available the published ALD and runway slope information for all LAHSO runway combinations at each airport of intended landing.

11. **Where are runway incursions most likely to occur?** (FAA-H-8083-25)

    Runway incursions most likely to cause accidents generally occur at complex, high-volume airports characterized by parallel/intersecting runways, multiple taxiway/runway intersections, complex taxi patterns, and the need for traffic to cross active runways. Historical data also shows that a large number of runway incursions involve general aviation pilots and often result from misunderstood controller instructions, confusion, disorientation, and/or inattention. Nearly all runway incursions are caused by human error.

12. If ATC instructs an aircraft to "taxi to" an assigned takeoff runway, does that authorize the aircraft to cross all runways that the taxi route intersects? (AIM 4-3-18)

No, a clearance must be obtained prior to crossing any runway. ATC will issue an explicit clearance for all runway crossings. When assigned a takeoff runway, ATC will first specify the runway, issue taxi instructions, and state any hold short instructions or runway crossing clearances if the taxi route will cross a runway.

13. What are several recommended practices concerning prevention of runway incursions? (FAA-H-8083-25)

a. Read back all runway crossing and/or hold short instructions.

b. Review airport layouts in preflight planning, before descending to land, and while taxiing as needed.

c. Know airport signage.

d. Review NOTAMs for runway/taxiway closures and construction area information.

e. Do not hesitate to request progressive taxi instructions from ATC when unsure of the taxi route.

f. Check for traffic before crossing any runway or entering a taxiway.

g. Turn on aircraft lights and rotating beacon or strobe lights while taxiing.

h. When landing, clear the active runway as quickly as possible, then wait for taxi instructions before further movement.

i. Study and use proper radio phraseology as described in the AIM in order to respond to and understand ground control instructions.

j. Write down complex taxi instructions at unfamiliar airports.

14. **What phraseology will an air traffic controller use to instruct a pilot to taxi onto the runway and await takeoff clearance?** (FAA Notice JO 7210.754)

    "Line Up and Wait" is now used instead of the previous "Taxi Into Position and Hold" instruction, in order to align with standard ICAO phraseology. The controller will state the call-sign, the departure runway and "Line Up and Wait" to instruct a pilot to enter the runway, line up, and wait for take-off clearance.

15. **Define the term "wind shear" and state the areas it is likely to occur.** (AC 00-6A)

    Wind shear is a change in wind speed and/or direction in a short distance resulting in a tearing or shearing effect, in a horizontal or vertical direction (occasionally in both). It may occur at any level in the atmosphere but three areas are of special concern:

    a. Wind shear with a low-level temperature inversion;

    b. Wind shear in a frontal zone or thunderstorm; and

    c. CAT at high levels associated with a jet stream or strong circulation.

16. **While flying a 3° glide slope, what conditions should the pilot expect concerning airspeed, pitch attitude, and altitude when encountering a windshear situation where a tailwind shears to a calm or headwind?** (AC 00-54)

    Pitch attitude .... Increases
    Required thrust................................ Reduced, then increases
    Vertical speed................................. Decreases, then increases
    Airspeed.. Increases, then decreases
    Reaction .... Reduce power initially, then increase

    Headwind increases
    eventually incres power

17. While flying a 3° glide slope, which conditions should the pilot expect concerning airspeed, pitch attitude, and altitude when encountering a windshear situation where a headwind shears to a calm or <u>tailwind</u>? (AC 00-54)

Pitch attitude .... Decreases

Required thrust.............................. Increases, then reduced

Vertical speed................................ Increases

Airspeed.. Decreases, then increases

Reaction .... Increase power, then a decrease in power

18. Concerning wind shear detection, what does the abbreviation "LLWAS" indicate? (AIM 4-3-7)

Low-Level Wind Shear Alert System (LLWAS), a computerized system that detects the presence of a possible hazardous low-level wind shear by continuously comparing the winds measured by sensors installed on the periphery of an airport with the wind measured at the center of the airport. If there is an excessive difference between the center field wind sensor and a peripheral wind sensor, a thunderstorm or thunderstorm gust front wind shear is possible.

19. What are "microbursts"? (AIM 7-1-26)

Microbursts are small-scale intense downdrafts that, upon reaching the surface, spread outward in all directions from the downdraft center. This causes both vertical and horizontal wind shears that can be extremely hazardous to all types and categories of aircraft, especially at low altitudes. Due to their small size, short life span, and the fact that they can occur over areas without surface precipitation, microbursts are not easily detectable using conventional weather radar or wind shear alert systems.

20. Where are microbursts most likely to occur? (AIM 7-1-26)

Microbursts can be found almost anywhere convective activity is present. They may be embedded in heavy rain associated with a thunderstorm, or in light rain in benign-appearing virga. When there is little or no precipitation at the surface accompanying the microburst, a ring of blowing dust may be the only visual clue of its existence.

21. What are some basic characteristics of a microburst? (AIM 7-1-26)

Size: Less than 1 mile in diameter as it descends from the cloud base; can extend $2\frac{1}{2}$ miles in diameter near ground level.

Intensity: Downdrafts as strong as 6,000 fpm; horizontal winds near the surface can be as strong as 45 knots resulting in a 90-knot wind shear (headwind to tailwind change for traversing aircraft).

Duration: An individual microburst will seldom last longer than 15 minutes from the time it strikes the ground until dissipation. Sometimes microbursts are concentrated into a line structure, and under these conditions activity may continue for as long as an hour.

22. How can microburst encounters be avoided? (AIM 7-1-26)

Pilots should heed wind shear PIREPs, as a previous pilot's encounter with a microburst may be the only indication received. However, since the wind shear intensifies rapidly in its early stages, a PIREP may not indicate the current severity of a microburst.

23. What is Clear Air Turbulence (CAT)? (AC 00-6A)

Turbulence encountered in air where no clouds are present; it is more commonly applied to high-level turbulence associated with wind shear. Cold outbreaks colliding with warm air from the south intensify weather systems in the vicinity of the jet stream, along the boundary between the cold and warm air. CAT develops in the turbulent energy exchange between the contrasting air masses.

24. Where is CAT encountered? (AC 00-6A)

CAT is often experienced in wind shears associated with sharply curved contours of strong lows, troughs, and ridges aloft, and in areas of strong cold or warm air advection. Also, mountain waves can create CAT. A common location of CAT is an upper trough on the cold (polar) side of the jet stream. Another frequent location is along the jet stream north and northeast of a rapidly deepening surface low.

CAT is most pronounced in winter when temperature contrast is greatest between cold and warm air. It can be encountered where there seems to be no reason for its occurrence because it drifts downwind from its main source region.

25. In flight planning, what weather information can be used in determining the location of CAT? (AC 00-45E)

Use of upper air charts and forecasts are of considerable help in locating CAT, because they are a source for determining jet stream location, wind shear, and most likely turbulence.

26. What procedure should be followed if CAT is inadvertently encountered? (AC 00-6A)

If caught in CAT not associated with a jet stream, your best bet is to change altitude, since you have no positive way of knowing in which direction the strongest shear lies. Maneuver gently when in turbulence to minimize stress on the airframe.

27. What is the best source of information on the location of CAT? (AIM 7-1-25)

The best source of information on CAT are PIREPs. Any pilot encountering CAT should report the time, location and intensity as soon as possible to that area's controlling facility (ATC, FSS, etc.).

28. What is meant by decompression? (FAA-H-8083-25)

Decompression is the inability of the aircraft's pressurization system to maintain the designed "aircraft cabin" pressure. For example, an aircraft is flying at an altitude of 29,000 feet but the aircraft cabin is pressurized to an altitude equivalent to 8,000 feet. If decompression occurs, the cabin pressure may become equivalent to that of the aircraft's altitude of 29,000 feet. The rate at which this occurs determines the severity of decompression.

29. What are the two types of decompression? (FAA-H-8083-25)

Explosive decompression—Cabin pressure decreases faster than the lungs can decompress; any kind of decompression occurring in less than $1/2$-second is usually considered explosive and potentially dangerous; can only be caused by structural damage, material failure, or by a door popping open.

Continued

Rapid decompression— A change in cabin pressure where the lungs decompress faster than the cabin; in this case, there is no likelihood of lung damage. Could be caused by a failure or malfunction in the pressurization system itself, or through slow leaks in the pressurized area.

30. What are the dangers of decompression? (FAA-H-8083-25)

a. Proper use of oxygen equipment must be accomplished quickly to avoid hypoxia. Unconsciousness may occur in a very short time. The time of useful consciousness (TUC) is considerably shortened when a person is subjected to a rapid decompression, which causes a rapid reduction of pressure on the body leading to a quick exhalation of the oxygen in the lungs.

b. At higher altitudes where the pressure differential is greater, being tossed or blown out of the airplane is a danger if one is near an opening during a decompression. Those who must be near an opening should always wear safety harnesses or seatbelts when in pressurized aircraft.

c. Evolved gas decompression sickness (the bends) is a danger.

d. Exposure to windblast and extreme cold is a danger.

31. Name the main types of icing an aircraft may encounter in flight. (AC 00-6)

Structural, induction system, and instrument icing.

32. What are the three types of structural icing that may occur in flight? (AC 00-6)

Clear ice— Forms when, after initial impact, the remaining liquid portion of the drop flows out over the aircraft surface and gradually freezes as a smooth sheet of solid ice; when drops are large as in rain or in cumuliform clouds.

Rime ice— Forms when drops are small, such as those in stratified clouds or light drizzle. The liquid portion remaining after initial impact freezes rapidly before the drop has time to spread over the aircraft surface. The small frozen droplets trap air between them giving the ice a white appearance.

Mixed ice—Forms when drops vary in size or when liquid drops are intermingled with snow or ice particles. It can form rapidly. Ice particles become imbedded in clear ice, building a very rough accumulation, sometimes in a mushroom shape on leading edges.

33. What condition(s) is/are necessary for structural icing to occur? (AC 00-6)

a. The aircraft must be flying through visible water such as rain or cloud droplets;

b. Temperature at the point where the moisture strikes the aircraft must be 0°C or colder.

Aerodynamic cooling can lower temperature of an airfoil to 0°C even though the ambient temperature is a few degrees warmer.

34. What is the definition of "freezing level" and how can you determine where that level is? (AC 00-6)

The freezing level is the lowest altitude in the atmosphere over a given location at which the air temperature reaches 0°C. It is possible to have multiple freezing layers when a temperature inversion occurs above the defined freezing level. A pilot should use icing forecasts as well as PIREPs to determine the approximate freezing level. Area forecasts, AIRMETs, SIGMETS, and Low-Level Significant Weather Charts are several examples of aviation weather products that contain icing information.

35. Which type of precipitation will produce the most hazardous icing conditions? (AC 00-6)

Freezing rain produces the most hazardous icing conditions.

36. In what outside air temperature ranges are the various types of ice likely to form? (AC 91-51)

Outside Air Temperature Range	Icing Type
0°C to -10°C	Clear
-10°C to -15°C	Mixed Clear and Rime
-15°C to -20°C	Rime

37. What is one significant severe icing hazard that pilots must be aware of when flying airplanes certified for flight in known icing? (AC 91-51)

A significant hazard of structural icing is the possible uncommanded and uncontrolled roll phenomenon referred to as "roll upset" that is associated with severe in-flight icing. Pilots flying airplanes certificated for flight in known icing conditions should be aware that severe icing is a condition *outside of* the airplane's certification icing envelope. Roll upset may be caused by airflow separation (aerodynamic stall) inducing self-deflection of the ailerons and loss of or degraded roll handling characteristics, and can result from severe icing conditions without the usual symptoms of ice accumulation or a perceived aerodynamic stall.

38. What is a tailplane (empennage) stall? (AC 91-51, 91-74)

A tailplane stall occurs when a tailplane, with accumulated ice, is placed at a sufficiently negative AOA and stalls. Since the tailplane counters the natural nose-down tendency caused by the center of lift of the main wing, the airplane will react by pitching down, sometimes uncontrollably, when the tailplane is stalled.

39. What changes in airplane configuration can aggravate a tailplane stall condition? (AC 91-74)

Most aircraft have a nose-down pitching moment from the wings because the CG is ahead of the center of pressure. The tailplane counteracts this moment by providing a downward force. The result of this configuration is the actions that move the wing away from stall, such as deployment of flaps or increasing speed, may increase the negative AOA of the tail. With ice on the tailplane, it may stall after full or partial deployment of flaps.

40. How can tailplane icing be detected? (AC 91-51)

Any of the following symptoms, occurring singly or in combination, may be a warning of tailplane icing:

a. Elevator control pulsing, oscillations, or vibrations;

b. Abnormal nose-down trim change;

c. Any other unusual or abnormal pitch anomalies (possibly resulting in pilot induced oscillations);

d. Reduction or loss of elevator effectiveness;

e. Sudden change in elevator force (control would move nose-down if unrestrained); and

f. Sudden uncommanded nose-down pitch.

41. How is recovery from a tailplane stall accomplished? (AC 91-51)

At the slightest indication of a tail stall, the pilot should:

a. Immediately retract the flaps to the previous setting and apply appropriate nose-up elevator pressure;

b. Increase airspeed appropriately for the reduced flap extension setting;

c. Apply sufficient power for aircraft configuration and conditions (high engine power settings may adversely impact response to tailplane stall conditions at high airspeed in some aircraft designs; observe the manufacturer's recommendations regarding power settings);

d. Make nose-down pitch changes slowly, even in gusting conditions, if circumstances allow; and

e. If a pneumatic deicing system is used, operate the system several times in an attempt to clear the tailplane of ice.

Remember: Recovery procedures from an ice-induced tailplane stall are opposite from those for an ice-induced wing stall.

42. What are the different icing intensity levels for airframe accumulation, and recommended pilot action for each? (AC 91-51)

a. *Trace:* Ice becomes perceptible. Rate of accumulation of ice is slightly greater than the rate of loss due to sublimation.
Pilot action: Unless encountered for one hour or more, deicing/anti-icing equipment and/or heading or altitude change not required.

b. *Light:* The rate of accumulation may create a problem if flying in this environment for one hour.
Pilot action: Deicing/anti-icing required occasionally to remove/prevent accumulation, or heading or altitude change required.

c. *Moderate:* The rate of accumulation is such that even short encounters become potentially hazardous.
Pilot action: Deicing/anti-icing required, or heading or altitude change required.

d. *Severe:* The rate of accumulation is such that deicing/anti-icing equipment fails to reduce or control the hazard.
Pilot action: Immediate heading or altitude change required.

F. Abnormal and Emergency Procedures

1. What are the two basic types of emergencies and what minimum conditions are suggested for declaring an emergency? (AIM 6-1-2)

An emergency can be either a *distress* or *urgency* condition: an aircraft is in at least an urgency condition the moment the pilot becomes doubtful about position, fuel endurance, weather, or any other condition that could adversely affect flight safety. Pilots should not hesitate to declare an emergency when they are faced with distress conditions such as fire, mechanical failure, or structural damage.

2. **What are several examples of abnormal or emergency situations?** (Order 8900.1)

   - Inflight fire
   - Smoke in cabin or cockpit
   - Rapid decompression
   - Emergency descent (with and without structural damage)
   - Hydraulic and electrical system failure or malfunctions
   - Landing gear and flap systems failure or malfunctions
   - Navigation or communications equipment failure

3. **Under what condition should a pilot operating under IFR advise ATC of "minimum fuel" status?** (AIM 5-5-15)

   Advise ATC of your minimum fuel status when your fuel supply has reached a state where, upon reaching the destination, you cannot accept any undue delay. This is merely an advisory that indicates an emergency situation is possible should any undue delay occur. Upon initial contact, the term "minimum fuel" should be used after stating the aircraft call sign.

4. **What are transponder codes 7500, 7600, and 7700 used for?** (AIM 6-2-2, 6-3-4, and 6-4-2)

   7500—Hijack in progress
   7600—Communications emergency
   7700—Emergency condition

5. **What are several examples of situations requiring the use of abnormal procedures checklists?**

   Used by flightcrews when dealing with situations other than emergencies; examples are flaps up landing, landing gear malfunction, ice protection system failure, inoperative generator, circuit breaker tripped, etc.

   These checklists may employ either the "challenge-do-verify" (CDV) method or the "do-verify" (DV) method. Depending on the abnormality, typically the non-flying pilot completes the abnormal procedures checklist while the flying pilot maintains control of the aircraft.

6. **All flight crewmembers must be familiar with the type, location, and purpose of each item of emergency equipment on board an aircraft. Give several examples of this equipment.** (Order 8900.1)

   Fire and oxygen bottles, first aid kits, life rafts, life preservers, crash axes, and emergency exits/lights. Also, familiarity with items of egress equipment such as slides, slide rafts, escape straps or handles, hatches, ladders or movable stairs should be included.

7. **What are some of the responsibilities of the airline flight crewmembers in the event an emergency evacuation of the aircraft becomes necessary?** (Order 8900.1)

   a. Recognize and act promptly in situations requiring an aircraft emergency evacuation.

   b. Use good judgment when there is a need to terminate aircraft evacuations.

   c. Communicate and coordinate throughout the evacuation process, until the evacuation is completed or terminated.

   d. Recognize when evacuation equipment is inoperative or faulty, prevent the use of such equipment, and divert egressing passengers to usable exits.

   e. Appropriate actions on aircraft equipped with auxiliary power units (APUs) that have a tendency to "torch."

   f. Manage passenger safety following unwarranted evacuations, especially after passengers have egressed from the aircraft and are on the ramp or taxiway.

G. Postflight

1. **What are some of the activities to be included in a postflight procedure?** (Order 8900.1)

   a. Coordination with ground crew on parking (marshalling, taxiing, or towing operations) and securing aircraft.

   b. All required placards in place.

   c. Appropriate flight crew/flight attendant trip paperwork completed.

   d. Determination of fuel remaining/additional fuel requirements.

   e. Postflight exterior inspection of aircraft.

   f. Appropriate logbook entries for required maintenance.

2. **When approaching or departing an aircraft, what are several items of concern that should be observed and evaluated by all flight crewmembers?** (Order 8900.1)

   a. *Ramp, apron, and taxiway surfaces*—general condition, cracks, holes, uneven surfaces.

   b. *Contamination debris*—FOD, fuel, oil, or hydraulic spills, snow and ice accumulations, taxi lines, gate markings, signs, signals.

   c. *Construction*—appropriate barriers, signs, markings, flags.

   d. *Vehicular operations*—conducted safely around aircraft and gate areas by qualified personnel.

Risk Management **4**

A. Aeronautical Decision Making (ADM)

1. What is the definition of the term "aeronautical decision making"? (AC 60-22)

It is the systematic approach to the mental process used by pilots to consistently determine the best course of action in response to a given set of circumstances.

2. What key principles are collectively called ADM? (FAA-H-8083-9)

Risk management, situational awareness and single-pilot/crew resource management.

3. What represents the first basic element in good decision making? (AC 60-22)

Situational awareness — a pilot with good situational awareness understands the dynamics of the flight environment and how they will affect the flight; this is also called "seeing the big picture."

4. Explain the three basic steps in the decision-making process. (FAA-H-8083-9)

a. Define the problem.

b. Choose a course of action.

c. Implement the decision and evaluate the outcome.

5. Which elements are involved in the DECIDE model for decision making? (AC 60-22)

D etect a change needing attention.

E stimate the need to counter or react to change.

C hoose the most desirable outcome for the flight.

I dentify actions to successfully control the change.

D o something to adapt to the change.

E valuate the effect of the action countering the change.

6. What are the six categories of the "I'M SAFE" personal checklist? (AC 60-22)

I llness
M edication
S tress
A lcohol
F atigue
E ating

7. Name the five hazardous attitudes that negatively impact a pilot's judgment and ability to make competent decisions, along with their antidotes. (AC 60-22)

Attitudes	Antidotes
Anti-authority	Follow the rules, they are usually right.
Impulsivity	Think first—Not so fast.
Invulnerability	It could happen to me.
Macho	Taking chances is foolish.
Resignation	I can make a difference, I am not helpless.

8. How does the 3P model of ADM help a pilot manage risk? (FAA-H-8083-9)

The 3P model offers a practical and structured way for a pilot to manage risk. The pilot:

- perceives the given set of circumstances for a flight (by identifying hazards in each risk category).
- processes by evaluating their impact on flight safety (what can hurt you).
- performs by implementing the best course of action (by changing the situation in your favor).

9. Most of the hazards in flying can be minimized by adopting what general philosophy? (AC 60-22)

Learn and adhere to published rules, procedures and recommendations.

B. CRM and SRM

1. What do the acronyms CRM and SRM refer to? (FAA-H-8081-5)

Crew Resource Management and Single-Pilot Resource Management refer to a pilot or flight crew's effective use of all available resources both onboard the aircraft and from outside sources, including human resources, hardware, and information.

2. Which groups routinely working with the cockpit crew or single pilot may also be viewed as essential participants in an effective CRM/SRM process? (FAA-H-8083-2)

The major contributors in the CRM/SRM process include, but are not limited to, pilots, dispatchers, cabin crew members, maintenance personnel, ATC, and passengers.

3. What are the five (5) focus points of CRM training? (AC 120-51)

CRM training focuses on situational awareness, communication skills, teamwork, task allocation, and decision-making.

4. What practical application provides a pilot with an effective method to practice SRM? (FAA-H-8083-2)

The 5 P checklist consists of the Plan, the Plane, the Pilot, the Passengers, and the Programming. It is based on the idea that the pilots have essentially five variables that impact their environment and can cause the pilot to make a single critical decision or several less critical decisions that when added together can create a critical outcome. A pilot should adopt a scheduled review of each of these critical variables at points in the flight where decisions are most likely to be effective.

5. An effective briefing, which is primarily a captain's responsibility, should address what points? (AC 120-51)

An effective briefing should address coordination, planning, and potential problems.

6. What is the purpose of Line-Oriented Flight Training (LOFT) or Special Purpose Operational Training (SPOT) for cockpit crewmembers? (AC 120-51)

Both LOFT and SPOT address appropriate responses with emphasis on situational awareness, inquiry/advocacy/assertion and crew coordination, when malfunctioning equipment, improper procedures, and adverse weather may reduce situational awareness.

7. What does the term "automation management" refer to? (FAA-H-8083-9)

Automation management is the demonstrated ability to control and navigate an aircraft by means of automated systems installed in the aircraft. The pilot must know what to expect, how to monitor the system for proper operation, and promptly take appropriate action if the system does not perform as expected.

8. What are SOPs? (AC 120-71)

Standard operating procedures (SOPs) are universally recognized as basic to safe aviation operations. Effective crew coordination and crew performance, two central concepts of CRM, depend upon the crew's having a shared mental model (founded on SOPs) of each task. SOPs should be clear, comprehensive, and readily available in the manuals used by flight deck crewmembers.

C. Situational Awareness

1. What is "situational awareness"? (FAA-H-8083-9)

Situational awareness is the accurate perception and understanding of all the factors and conditions within the four fundamental risk elements affecting safety before, during, and after the flight.

2. Situational awareness takes into consideration which four elements? (FAA-H-8083-9)

To maintain situational awareness, an accurate perception must be attained of how the **P**ilot, **A**ircraft, en**V**ironment, and **E**xternal pressures (PAVE) combine to affect the flight.

3. **What are some of the elements, both inside and outside the aircraft, that a pilot must consider in order to maintain situational awareness?** (FAA-H-8083-9)

Inside aircraft—status of aircraft systems, pilots, and passengers.

Outside aircraft—environmental conditions of the flight, spatial orientation of the aircraft, relationship to surrounding terrain, traffic, weather and airspace.

4. **What are some of the obstacles to maintaining situational awareness?** (FAA-H-8083-9)

Fatigue, stress, and work overload can cause the pilot to fixate on a single perceived important item rather than maintaining an overall awareness of the flight situation. A contributing factor in many accidents is a distraction that diverts the pilot's attention from monitoring the instruments or scanning outside the aircraft. Many cockpit distractions begin as a minor problem, such as a gauge that is not reading correctly, but result in accidents as the pilot diverts attention to the perceived problem and neglects to properly control the aircraft.

5. **A majority of CFIT accidents have been attributed to what factors?** (AC 61-134)

Risk factors include: lack of pilot currency, loss of situational awareness, pilot distractions and breakdown of SRM, failure to comply with minimum safe altitudes, breakdown in effective ADM, and insufficient planning, especially for the descent and arrival segments.

6. **What are "operational pitfalls"?** (FAA-H-8083-9)

These are classic behavioral traps into which pilots have been known to fall. Particularly pilots with considerable experience as a rule strive to complete a flight as planned, please passengers, meet schedules, and generally demonstrate that they have the "right stuff." The basic drive to demonstrate the right stuff can have an adverse effect on safety, and can impose an unrealistic assessment of piloting skills under stressful conditions. These tendencies ultimately can bring about dangerous and often illegal practices, which may lead to a mishap.

7. **What are some examples of operational pitfalls that pilots have been known to experience?** (FAA-H-8083-9)

   a. Peer pressure

   b. Mind set

   c. Get-There-Itis

   d. Duck-Under Syndrome/descent below minimums

   e. Scud running

   f. Continuing VFR into instrument conditions

   g. Getting behind the aircraft

   h. Loss of positional or situational awareness

   i. Operating without adequate fuel reserves

   j. Descent below the minimum enroute altitude

   k. Flying outside the envelope

   l. Neglect of flight planning, preflight inspections, and checklists

D. Use of Checklists

1. **What is a flow check?** (Order 8900.1)

   A method by which each pilot scans the various cockpit panels in a sequential pattern or flow. During the scan, the pilot will test, check, and set all switches and indicators, starting at a specific cockpit panel location and working their way through to completion. After completion of the flow check, the pilot will use the checklist to ensure all steps are complete. This method allows the flight crew to use flow patterns from memory to accomplish a series of actions quickly and efficiently. Each individual crewmember can work independently which helps balance the workload between crewmembers.

2. **What is a "challenge and response" checklist?** (Order 8900.1)

   Also known as the "challenge, do, verify" method, it consists of a crewmember making a challenge before an action is initiated, taking the action, and then verifying that the action item has been accomplished. It is most effective when one crewmember issues the challenge and the second crewmember takes the action and responds to the first crewmember, verifying that the action was taken. This method requires that the checklist be accomplished methodically, one item at a time, in an unvarying sequence. The primary advantage is the deliberate and systematic manner in which each action item must be accomplished: it keeps all crewmembers involved (in the loop), provides for concurrence from a second crewmember before an action is taken and positive confirmation that the action was accomplished.

The disadvantages of this method are that it is rigid and inflexible and that crewmembers cannot accomplish different tasks at the same time.

3. What are some examples of the various checklists airline crews use in the course of a flight?

a. *Before Start*—checked after preflight is complete and all flight crewmembers are on board and ready. It can include additional items if it is the aircraft's first flight of the day.

b. *After Start*—checked after engine start; ensures all systems are operating normally.

c. *Before Takeoff*—checked during taxi or while holding on taxiway waiting for takeoff clearance. Usually includes a pre-takeoff briefing by the captain.

d. *Cleared for Takeoff*—completed when cleared for takeoff. Quick final check of critical systems (i.e., flaps set, autofeather on, etc.) as well as critical speeds for takeoff (V_1, V_R, V_2).

e. *After Takeoff*—checked after takeoff during initial climb; completed as soon as workload permits. Includes items such as pressurization check, climb power set, etc.

f. *Cruise*—checked when leveling off at cruise altitude. Includes setting power and props, checking instruments, checking pressurization, passenger announcement.

g. *Descent and Approach*—completed when leaving cruise altitude in preparation for an approach. Includes an approach brief by the pilot flying (PF), passenger briefing, final systems check, and configuring aircraft for approach.

Continued

h. *Before Landing* — completed prior to FAF for approach. Aircraft is configured and stabilized for final approach; usually consists of several short checklists that occur prior to FAF, at FAF, prior to 500 feet AGL, at 500 feet AGL, and immediately prior to landing.

i. *After Landing* — checked after clearing the runway. Includes items such as flaps up, transponder standby, radar off, external lights as required, APU start.

j. *Shutdown* — occurs after aircraft has come to a complete stop, and parking brake is set. Includes securing of all systems in the proper sequence. Additional items may be added if it is the aircraft's last flight of the day.

4. What is the significance of "immediate action items" found on some checklists? (Order 8900.1)

An immediate action item (also known as a memory item) is an action that must be accomplished so expeditiously (in order to avoid or stabilize a hazardous situation) that time is not available for a crewmember to refer to a manual or checklist. Crewmembers must be so familiar with these actions that they can perform them correctly and reliably from memory. Situations that require immediate action include, but are not limited to the following:

a. Imminent threat of crewmember incapacitation,

b. Imminent threat of loss of aircraft control,

c. Imminent threat of destruction of a system or component that makes continued safety of the flight and subsequent landing improbable.

5. Why do emergency checklists require the pilots to "call for checklist" after completion of the immediate action items? (Order 8900.1)

After completion of the immediate action items, and the emergency has been brought under control, the pilot should call for the actual checklist, so as to verify that all initial immediate action items on the emergency checklist were accomplished. Only after this is done should the remainder of the checklist be completed. This procedure ensures that the emergency is dealt with quickly and efficiently and that all immediate action items are completed first.

6. What is the function of "standard callouts" made by flight crews? (Order 8900.1)

Standard callouts for basic operations should be established to ensure that the flight crew functions as a well-coordinated team and maintains the situational awareness necessary for safe operation of the aircraft. The pilot not flying (PNF) should be assigned the responsibility for monitoring the flight progress and for providing callouts to the pilot flying (PF) for each significant transition point, event, or failure condition.

7. What are examples of standard callouts for basic IFR operations? (Order 8900.1)

a. During climb to assigned altitude, the PNF should provide a callout when passing through the transition altitude (as a reminder to reset the altimeters) and when approaching 1,000 feet below assigned altitude.

b. During cruise, the PNF should provide a callout when the aircraft altitude deviates by 200 feet or more from the assigned altitude.

c. During descent from enroute flight altitude to initial approach altitude, the PNF should provide a callout when approaching 1,000 feet above the assigned altitude, an altitude where a speed reduction is required (e.g. 10,000 feet in the U.S.), 1,000 feet above the initial approach altitude (above field elevation for approaches in VFR conditions), and when passing the transition level.

8. What are examples of standard callouts for IFR Category I approaches? (Order 8900.1)

a. *Beginning the final approach segment*—prior to this, a callout should be provided to cross-check the altimeter settings and instrument indications and to confirm the status of warning flags for the flight and navigation instruments and other critical systems.

b. *Rate of descent callouts*—If the flight altitude is less than 2,000 feet above ground level (AGL), the PNF should provide a callout when the rate of descent exceeds 2,000 feet per minute.

Continued

Additionally, a callout should be provided when the rate of descent exceeds 1,000 fpm if the flight altitude is less than 1,000 feet AGL.

c. *Altitude callouts*—the PNF should provide a callout at 1,000 feet above the landing elevation to confirm aircraft configuration and to cross-check the flight and navigation instruments. For approaches conducted in IFR conditions, the PNF should also provide a callout at 100 feet above the MDA or DH (as applicable) followed by a callout upon arriving at the MDA or DH.

d. *Airspeed callouts*—the PNF should provide a callout at any point in the approach when the airspeed is below the planned speed for the existing aircraft configuration. If the aircraft has entered the final approach segment, a callout should also be provided when the airspeed exceeds 10 knots above the planned final approach speed.

e. *Visual cue callouts*—the PNF should provide a callout when the visual cues required to continue the approach by visual reference are acquired, such as "approach lights" or "runway." This callout should not be made unless the available visual cues meet the requirements of 14 CFR §91.116 for descent below the MDA or DH.

f. *Destabilized approach callouts*—any time approach becomes destabilized (approach criteria not met). The approach is destabilized if the criteria for a "stabilized approach" are not met and maintained.

g. *Approach profile callouts*—the PNF should provide a callout if the aircraft deviates from the proper approach profile during any portion of an instrument approach.

9. **What additional callouts should be made during the final approach segment of an instrument approach procedure?** (Order 8900.1)

   a. The PNF should provide a callout if the aircraft has entered the final approach segment of an ILS/MLS approach and the localizer (azimuth) displacement exceeds 1/3 dot and/or the glide-slope (elevation) displacement is greater than one dot.

   b. For localizer (azimuth) based approaches, a callout should be made if the displacement exceeds 1/3 dot during the final approach segment.

   c. For VOR based approaches, a callout should be made if the displacement exceeds 2 degrees during the final approach segment.

   d. For NDB based approaches, a callout should be made if the displacement exceeds 5 degrees during this segment.

10. **What information should be covered in the takeoff/ departure and approach/landing briefings?** (FAA-H-8081-5)

    If the operator or aircraft manufacturer has not specified a briefing, the briefing must cover appropriate items, such as: departure runway, DP/STAR/IAP, power settings, speeds, abnormal or emergency procedures prior to or after reaching decision speed (i.e., V_1 or V_{MC}), emergency return intentions, missed approach procedures, FAF, altitude at FAF, initial rate of descent, DA/DH/MDA, time to missed approach, and what is expected of the other crewmembers during the takeoff/DP and approach/landing.

Regulations 5

A. 14 CFR Part 1

1. What type of information can be found in Part 1?
(14 CFR Part 1)

Part 1 contains general definitions, abbreviations and symbols, and rules of construction used throughout Title 14 of the Code of Federal Regulations.

2. Define the term "air carrier." (14 CFR Part 1)

An "air carrier" is a person who undertakes directly by lease, or other arrangement, to engage in air transportation.

3. Define the term "commercial operator." (14 CFR Part 1)

A person who, for compensation or hire, engages in the carriage by aircraft in air commerce of persons or property, other than as an air carrier or foreign air carrier or under the authority of 14 CFR Part 375. Where it is doubtful that an operation is for "compensation or hire," the test applied is whether the carriage by air is merely incidental to the person's other business or is, in itself, a major enterprise for profit.

4. What is the definition of "crewmember"? (14 CFR Part 1)

A crewmember is a person assigned to perform duty in an aircraft during flight time.

5. When does a pilot's "flight time" begin and end?
(14 CFR Part 1)

A pilot's "flight time" commences when an aircraft moves under its own power for the purpose of flight and ends when the aircraft comes to rest after landing.

6. With respect to aircraft, define "operate." (14 CFR Part 1)

"Operate" means to use, cause to use, or authorize to use an aircraft for the purpose of air navigation including the piloting of aircraft, with or without the right of legal control (as owner, lessee, or otherwise).

7. **What does the term "operational control" refer to?**
(14 CFR Part 1)

The term "operational control" with respect to a flight, means the exercise of authority over initiating, conducting or terminating a flight.

B. 14 CFR Part 61

1. **What is a Category II or III ILS pilot authorization?**
(14 CFR §61.13)

A letter of authorization that is part of an applicant's instrument rating or airline transport pilot certificate allowing a pilot/operator, with the required training and equipment, to conduct approaches to a lower DH and visibility. Upon original issue, the authorization contains the following limitations:

a. For Category II operations, the limitation is 1,600 feet RVR and a 150-foot decision height; and

b. For Category III operations, each initial limitation is specified in the authorization document.

2. **When may a Category II or III limitation be removed?**
(14 CFR §61.13)

a. In the case of Category II limitations, a limitation is removed when the holder shows that, since the beginning of the sixth preceding month, the holder has made three Category II ILS approaches with a 150-foot decision height to a landing under actual or simulated instrument conditions.

b. In the case of Category III limitations, a limitation is removed as specified in the authorization.

3. **Unless otherwise authorized, when would a pilot be required to hold a type rating?** (14 CFR §61.31)

A person who acts as a pilot-in-command of any of the following aircraft must hold a type rating for that aircraft:

a. Large aircraft (except lighter-than-air).

b. Turbojet-powered airplane.

c. Other aircraft specified by the Administrator through aircraft type certificate procedures.

4. When may a pilot log flight time as second-in-command time? (14 CFR §61.51)

A pilot may log second-in-command time only for that flight time during which that person:

a. Is qualified in accordance with the second-in-command requirements of §61.55 and occupies a crewmember station in an aircraft that requires more than one pilot by the aircraft's type certificate; or

b. Holds the appropriate category, class, and instrument rating (if an instrument rating is required for the flight) for the aircraft being flown, and more than one pilot is required under the type certification of the aircraft or the regulations under which the flight is being conducted.

5. To satisfy the minimum required instrument experience for IFR operations in an airplane, a pilot must accomplish what actions within the preceding six months? (14 CFR §61.57)

Within the 6 calendar months preceding the month of the flight, that person must have performed and logged at least the following tasks and iterations in an airplane for the instrument rating privileges to be maintained in actual weather conditions, or under simulated conditions using a view-limiting device that involves having performed the following:

a. Six instrument approaches.

b. Holding procedures and tasks.

c. Intercepting and tracking courses through the use of navigational electronic systems.

6. What privileges are given to an ATP? (14 CFR §61.167)

A person who holds an airline transport pilot certificate is entitled to the same privileges as those afforded a person who holds a commercial pilot certificate with an instrument rating.

7. What restriction is imposed on an ATP regarding instruction of other pilots in air transportation service? (14 CFR §61.167)

An airline pilot may not instruct in aircraft, flight simulators, and flight training devices for more than 8 hours in any 24-concecutive-hour period, or for more than 36 hours in any 7-consecutive-day period.

C. 14 CFR Part 117

Editorial note: This new regulation is pending at the time of press; the final rule is expected August 2011. Visit the Reader Resources webpage for updated information: **www.asa2fly.com/reader/oegatp**

1. What is 14 CFR Part 117? (14 CFR §117.1)

Part 117 prescribes the flight and duty limitations and rest requirements for all flightcrew members and certificate holders conducting operations under 14 CFR Part 121. This regulation also applies to all flightcrew members and Part 121 certificate holders when conducting flights under 14 CFR Part 91.

2. What is the definition of "fatigue"? (14 CFR §117.3)

Fatigue means a physiological state of reduced mental or physical performance capability resulting from lack of sleep or increased physical activity that can reduce a crewmember's alertness and ability to safely operate an aircraft or perform safety-related duties.

3. Define the term "flight duty period." (14 CFR §117.3)

Flight duty period (FDP) means a period that begins when a flightcrew member is required to report for duty with the intention of conducting a flight, a series of flights, or positioning or ferrying flights, and ends when the aircraft is parked after the last flight and there is no intention for further aircraft movement by the same flightcrew member. A flight duty period includes deadhead transportation before a flight segment without an intervening required rest period, training conducted in an aircraft, flight simulator or flight training device, and airport/standby reserve.

4. Define the term "rest period." (14 CFR §117.3)

Rest period means a continuous period determined prospectively during which the crewmember is free from all restraint by the certificate holder, including freedom from present responsibility for work, should the occasion arise.

5. What is the definition of an "augmented flight crew"? (14 CFR §117.3)

An "augmented flight crew" is one that has more than the minimum number of flight crewmembers required by the airplane type certificate to operate the aircraft, in order to allow a flight crewmember to be replaced by another qualified flight crewmember for in-flight rest.

6. Who has the responsibility for ensuring that each flight crewmember is rested and working the correct number of hours? (14 CFR §117.5)

It is the joint responsibility of the certificate holder and the flight crewmember.

7. How many maximum flight duty period hours are allowed for un-augmented operations? Augmented operations? (14 CFR §117.15, 117.19)

Un-augmented: 9 to 13 FDP hours based on start time and the number of flight segments.
Augmented: 12 to 18 FDP hours based on start time, rest facility, number of pilots.

8. Maximum flight duty period hours for augmented and un-augmented flight crewmembers are based on what variables? (14 CFR §117.15–117.19)

Maximum FDP hours are based on the number of flight segments, the time of start (home base or acclimated to time zone), type of rest facility, and number of pilots.

9. **What are the 28 and 365 consecutive calendar day cumulative duty limitations on the amount of "flight time" a pilot may be assigned?** (14 CFR §117.23)

   100 hours in any 28 consecutive calendar day period, and 1,000 hours in any 365 consecutive calendar day period.

10. **What are the 168 and 672 consecutive hour cumulative duty limitations on the amount of "flight duty period" hours a pilot may be assigned?** (14 CFR §117.23)

    60 flight duty period hours in any 168 consecutive hours (7 days); 190 flight duty period hours in any 672 consecutive hours (28 days).

11. **What minimum number of "rest period" hours must be given to a pilot prior to assignment of a flight duty period?** (14 CFR §117.25)

    No certificate holder may schedule and no flightcrew member may accept an assignment for reserve or a flight duty period unless the flightcrew member is given a rest period of at least 9 consecutive hours before beginning the reserve or flight duty period.

12. **How is a pilot's "rest period" measured?** (14 CFR §117.25)

    It is measured from the time the flightcrew member reaches the hotel or other suitable accommodation.

13. **What is the minimum number of consecutive hours a pilot must be free from all duty in any 168 consecutive hour period?** (14 CFR §117.25)

    Before beginning any reserve or flight duty period, a flightcrew member must be given at least 30 consecutive hours free from all duty in any 168 consecutive hours (7 day) period.

14. **Are there any exceptions that would affect the total required crew rest period hours?** (14 CFR §117.25)

    a. Crossing more than 4 time zones during a series of flight duty periods that exceeds 168 consecutive hours.

    b. A flight crewmember operating in a new theater.

c. In the event of unforeseen circumstances, the PIC and certificate holder may reduce the rest period from a 9 to an 8-consecutive-hour rest period.

15. Is time spent "deadheading" considered rest time? (14 CFR §117.29)

No; All time spent in deadhead transportation is considered part of a duty period.

D. 14 CFR Part 119

1. What operations are governed by 14 CFR Part 119? (14 CFR §119.1, Order 8900.1)

Part 119 establishes the general certification requirements for air carriers and commercial operators. It contains the following provisions:

a. Definitions appropriate to air operator certification.

b. Roadmap to determine the appropriate operating rules (part 121, 125, or 135) for the kind of operations.

c. Common certification requirements for Parts 121 and 135 (i.e. OpSpecs, management personnel).

d. Miscellaneous safety provisions common to Parts 121 and 135 (i.e., wet leasing, emergency operations).

2. What are the two basic types of air operator certificates issued to U.S. applicants who will conduct operations in common carriage? (14 CFR §119.5)

a. *Air Carrier Certificate* — this certificate is issued to applicants who plan to conduct interstate, foreign, or overseas transportation, or to carry mail.

b. *Operating Certificate* — this certificate is issued to applicants who plan to conduct intrastate transportation.

3. What is the document that authorizes an air carrier or commercial operator to operate within a specific geographic area? (14 CFR §119.7)

The Operations Specifications, or OpSpecs.

4. **The Operations Specifications for an air carrier or commercial operator contain what type of information?** (14 CFR §119.7, FAA-H-8261-1)

OpSpecs define the appropriate authorizations, limitations, and procedures based on the type of operation, equipment, and qualifications of the airline/commercial operator. They can be adjusted to accommodate variables including aircraft and aircraft equipment, operator capabilities, and changes in aviation technology.

5. **Are the Operations Specifications regulatory, for an air carrier or commercial operator?** (FAA-H-8261-1)

The Operations Specifications are an extension of the CFR, making them a legal, binding contract between a properly certificated air transportation organization and the FAA for compliance with the CFRs applicable to their operation.

6. **What are several examples of "for-hire" type operations that do not require air carrier or commercial operator certification?** (14 CFR §119.1)

Student instruction, certain types of non-stop commercial air tours, ferry or training flights, aerial work operations (crop dusting, banner towing, aerial photography, fire fighting, helicopter operations in construction or repair work, powerline or pipeline patrol), hot air balloon sightseeing flights, etc.

E. 14 CFR Part 121

1. **Who must the crew of a domestic or flag air carrier airplane be able to communicate with, under normal conditions, along the entire route of flight?** (14 CFR §121.99)

A two-way radio communication system or other approved means of communication is available between each airplane and the appropriate dispatch office, and between each airplane and the appropriate air traffic control unit.

2. **What effective runway length is required for a turbojet powered airplane at the destination airport if the runways are forecast to be wet or slippery at the ETA?** (14 CFR §121.195)

115 percent of the runway length required for a dry runway.

3. **When must the emergency lights on a passenger-carrying airplane be armed or turned on?** (14 CFR §121.310)

The emergency lights must be armed or turned on during taxiing, takeoff, and landing.

4. **A crewmember interphone system is required on which airplane?** (14 CFR §121.319)

No person may operate an airplane with a seating capacity of more than 19 passengers unless the airplane is equipped with a crewmember interphone system.

5. **What is the passenger oxygen supply requirement for a flight, in a turbine-powered aircraft, with a cabin pressure altitude in excess of 15,000 feet?** (14 CFR §121.329)

There must be enough oxygen available for each passenger carried during the entire flight at those altitudes.

6. **What are the pilot supplemental oxygen requirements for emergency descent of turbine-engine-powered airplanes with pressurized cabins?** (14 CFR §121.333)

At flight altitudes above 10,000 feet, a minimum of a 2-hour supply of supplemental oxygen must be provided for each flight crewmember on flight deck duty.

At flight altitudes above FL250, if it becomes necessary for one pilot to leave his/her duty station, the remaining pilot shall put on and use an oxygen mask until the other pilot has returned to the duty station. Exception: one pilot need not wear and use an oxygen mask if each flight crewmember on flight deck duty has a quick-donning type of oxygen mask. A flight crewmember must be able to put on and start using a quick-donning oxygen mask within 5 seconds.

7. For the purposes of testing a flight recorder system, how much data may be erased? (14 CFR §121.343)

A total of 1 hour of the oldest recorded data may be erased for the purpose of testing the flight recorder or the flight recorder system.

8. What are the airborne weather radar equipment requirements for air carriers? (14 CFR §121.357)

No person may dispatch an airplane (or begin the flight of an airplane in the case of a certificate holder that does not use a dispatch system) under IFR or night VFR conditions when current weather reports indicate that thunderstorms, or other potentially hazardous weather conditions that can be detected with airborne weather radar, may reasonably be expected along the route to be flown, unless the airborne weather radar equipment is in satisfactory operating condition.

If the airborne weather radar becomes inoperative en route, the airplane must be operated in accordance with the approved instructions and procedures specified in the operations manual for such an event.

9. When must the cockpit voice recorder be on and operative? (14 CFR §121.359)

The cockpit voice recorder must be operated continuously from the start of the "before starting engine" checklist to completion of final checklist upon flight termination.

10. What is the minimum number of flight attendants required on an airplane having the following seating capacities: 30, 70, 120? (14 CFR §121.391)

For airplanes having a seating capacity of:

9 to 50—one flight attendant
51 to 100—two flight attendants
101 to 150—three flight attendants

For airplanes having a seating capacity of more than 100 passengers—two flight attendants plus one additional flight attendant for each unit (or part of a unit) of 50 passenger seats above a seating capacity of 100 passengers.

11. **Define the following types of training: initial, transition, upgrade, differences.** (14 CFR §121.400)

    Initial training — Required for crewmembers and dispatchers who have not qualified and served in the same capacity on another airplane of the same group.

    Transition training — Required for crewmembers and dispatchers who have qualified and served in the same capacity on another airplane of the same group.

    Upgrade training — Required for crewmembers who have qualified and served as second-in-command or flight engineer on a particular airplane type, before they serve as pilot-in-command or second-in-command, respectively, on that airplane.

    Differences training — Required for crewmembers and dispatchers who have qualified and served on a particular type airplane, when the Administrator finds differences training is necessary before a crewmember serves in the same capacity on a particular variation of that airplane.

12. **How often must a crewmember actually operate the airplane emergency equipment after initial training?** (14 CFR §121.417)

    Every 24 calendar months.

13. **What are the requirements that must be met by an airline pilot to re-establish recency of experience?** (14 CFR §121.439)

    A required pilot flight crewmember must have made
    - 3 takeoffs and landings within the preceding 90 days in type.
    - 1 takeoff with a simulated failure of the most critical powerplant.
    - 1 landing from an ILS approach to the lowest ILS minimums authorized for the certificate holder.
    - 1 landing to a full stop.

14. **What are the line check requirements for the pilot-in-command of a domestic air carrier?** (14 CFR §121.440)

Within the preceding 12 calendar months, the PIC must have passed a line check in which they satisfactorily perform the duties and responsibilities of a pilot-in-command in one of the types of airplanes they are to fly.

15. **How often must a pilot-in-command complete a proficiency check?** (14 CFR §121.441)

A pilot-in-command must complete a proficiency check within the preceding 12 calendar months, and in addition, within the preceding 6 calendar months, either a proficiency check or simulator training.

16. **How often must a pilot flight crewmember other than a pilot-in-command complete a proficiency check or line-oriented training?** (14 CFR §121.441)

The pilot must have received either a proficiency check or a line-oriented simulator training course within the preceding 24 calendar months.

17. **Briefly describe the flight time limitations for flight crews of domestic operations.** (14 CFR §121.471)

No certificate holder conducting domestic operations may schedule any flight crewmember and no flight crewmember may accept an assignment for flight time in scheduled air transportation or in other commercial flying if that crewmember's total flight time in all commercial flying will exceed:

a. 1,000 hours in any calendar year;

b. 100 hours in any calendar month;

c. 30 hours in any 7 consecutive days;

d. 8 hours between required rest periods.

18. **Briefly describe the basic rest requirements for flight crews of domestic operations.** (14 CFR §121.471)

No certificate holder conducting domestic operations may schedule a flight crewmember and no flight crewmember may accept an assignment for flight time during the 24 consecutive hours preceding the scheduled completion of any flight segment without a scheduled rest period during that 24 hours of at least the following:

a. 9 consecutive hours of rest for less than 8 hours of scheduled flight time.

b. 10 consecutive hours of rest for 8 or more, but less than 9 hours of scheduled flight time.

c. 11 consecutive hours of rest for 9 or more hours of scheduled flight time.

d. 24 consecutive hours during any 7 consecutive days.

Note: A certificate holder may schedule a flight crewmember for less than the rest required or may reduce a scheduled rest under specific conditions. *See* 14 CFR §121.471.

19. **How does deadhead transportation, going to or from a duty assignment, affect the computation of flight time limits for air carrier flight crewmembers?** (14 CFR §121.491)

Time spent in deadhead transportation to or from a duty assignment is not considered to be part of a rest period.

20. **With regard to flight crewmember duties, what operations are considered to be in the "critical phase of flight"?** (14 CFR §121.542)

Critical phases of flight include all ground operations involving taxi, takeoff and landing, and all other flight operations conducted below 10,000 feet, except cruise flight. No flight crewmember may engage in, nor may any pilot-in-command permit, any activity during a critical phase that could distract any flight crewmember from the performance of his or her duties or interfere in any way with the proper conduct of those duties.

21. What action shall the pilot-in-command take if it becomes necessary to shut down one of the two engines on an air carrier airplane? (14 CFR §121.565)

The pilot-in-command shall land at the nearest suitable airport (in reference to time, not distance) at which a safe landing can be made.

22. A domestic air carrier flight has a delay while on the ground at an intermediate airport. How long is it before a re-dispatch release is required? (14 CFR §121.593)

Except when an airplane lands at an intermediate airport specified in the original dispatch release and remains there for not more than one hour, no person may start a flight unless an aircraft dispatcher specifically authorizes that flight.

23. When is a takeoff alternate airport required for departure? (14 CFR §121.617)

If the weather conditions at the airport of takeoff are below the landing minimums in the certificate holder's operations specifications for that airport, no person may dispatch or release an aircraft from that airport unless the dispatch or flight release specifies an alternate airport located within the following distances from the airport of takeoff:

a. Aircraft having two engines — not more than one hour from the departure airport at normal cruising speed in still air with one engine inoperative.

b. Aircraft having three or more engines — not more than two hours from the departure airport at normal cruising speed in still air with one engine inoperative.

24. **When is an alternate airport required for the destination airport?** (14 CFR §121.619)

No person may dispatch an airplane under IFR or over the top unless there is at least one alternate airport for each destination airport in the dispatch release. When the weather conditions forecast for the destination and first alternate airport are marginal, at least one additional alternate must be designated. However, no alternate airport is required if, for at least 1 hour before and 1 hour after the estimated time of arrival at the destination airport, the appropriate weather reports or forecasts, or any combination of them, indicate:

a. The ceiling will be at least 2,000 feet above the airport elevation; and

b. Visibility will be at least 3 miles.

25. **What are the minimum weather conditions that must exist for an airport to be listed as an alternate airport in the dispatch release for a domestic air carrier?** (14 CFR §121.625)

No person may list an airport as an alternate airport in the dispatch or flight release unless the appropriate weather reports or forecasts, or any combination thereof, indicate that the weather conditions will be at or above the alternate weather minimums specified in the certificate holder's operations specifications for that airport when the flight arrives.

26. **If an airport is not listed in a domestic air carrier's operations specifications and does not have the prescribed takeoff minimums, what will the minimum weather conditions be for takeoff?** (14 CFR §121.637)

No pilot may takeoff an airplane from an airport that is not listed in the operations specifications unless the weather conditions at that airport are equal to or better than the weather minimums for takeoff prescribed in Part 97. Where minimums are not prescribed for the airport, the weather minimums of 800–2, 900–1-1/2, or 1,000–1 are required.

27. What is the reserve fuel requirement for a domestic air carrier airplane? (14 CFR §121.639)

No person may dispatch or takeoff an airplane unless it has enough fuel to fly to the airport to which it is dispatched, and to fly to and land at the most distant alternate airport (where required) for the airport to which dispatched and thereafter, to fly for 45 minutes at normal cruising fuel consumption.

28. Under what conditions may an air carrier pilot continue an instrument approach to the DH, after receiving a weather report indicating that less than minimum published landing conditions exist at the airport? (14 CFR §121.651)

When the weather report is received after the pilot has begun the final approach segment of the instrument approach.

29. If the pilot-in-command's flight time in a particular type airplane is less than 100 hours, what effect will that have on landing minimums? (14 CFR §121.652)

The minimums for the destination airport must be increased by 100 feet and 1/2 statute mile.

30. What information must be contained in, or attached to, the dispatch release for a domestic air carrier flight? (14 CFR §121.687)

It must contain at least the following information concerning each flight:

a. aircraft identification number;

b. trip number;

c. departure airport, intermediate stops, destination airports, and alternate airports;

d. a statement of the type of operation;

e. minimum fuel supply; and

f. current weather information.

g. ETOPS diversion time, if flight is dispatched as an ETOPS.

31. What documents are required to be carried on board a domestic air carrier flight? (14 CFR §121.695)

The pilot-in-command of an airplane shall carry in the airplane, to its destination, a copy of the completed load manifest (or information from it, except information concerning cargo and passenger distribution), a copy of the dispatch release and a copy of the flight plan.

F. 14 CFR Part 125

1. What is 14 CFR Part 125? (14 CFR §125.3, AC 125-1)

Part 125 regulations establish a uniform set of certification and operational rules for large airplanes having a seating capacity of 20 or more passengers or a maximum payload capacity of 6,000 pounds or more, when used for private carriage. These rules substantially upgrade the level of safety applicable to large airplanes formerly operated under Part 91.

2. What operations are permitted when operating under Part 125 regulations? (Order 8900.1)

Large aircraft engaged in "private carriage" operations in which persons or cargo are transported without compensation for hire. Examples of these type operations are private or corporate operators carrying company personnel, property and guest, including cost sharing under 14 CFR §91.501(d), or historic (museum or collection) flight operations.

Note: Part 125 provides for the operation of large aircraft that are not conducting "common carriage" operations. Non-common carriage for hire operations are allowed, but should be reviewed carefully to verify that the operation is not "common carriage". Operators are not permitted to "hold out" directly or indirectly.

3. Define the terms "private carriage" and "common carriage." (AC 120-12)

Private carriage — is carriage for hire which does not involve "holding out."

Common carriage — refers to the carriage of passengers or cargo as a result of advertising the availability of the carriage to the public. A carrier becomes a common carrier when it "holds itself out" to the public, or a segment of the public, as a willing to furnish transportation within the limits of its facilities to any person who wants it. There are four elements in defining a common carrier: (1) a holding out of a willingness to (2) transport persons or property (3) from place to place (4) for compensation.

4. Give several examples of "holding out" to the public. (AC 125-1)

Advertising through telephone yellow pages, billboards, television, radio, individual ticketing, etc. are examples that have been legally found to be "holding out." Part 125 prohibits certificate holders from conducting any operation which results directly or indirectly from holding out to the general public.

G. 14 CFR Part 135

1. What type of manual is a Part 135 certificate holder required to provide and maintain? (14 CFR §135.21)

Each certificate holder shall prepare and keep current, a manual setting forth the procedures and policies acceptable to the administrator. The manual must be used by the certificate holder's maintenance, flight, and ground personnel in conducting operations. The certificate holder shall maintain at least one copy of the manual at its principal base of operations. A copy of the manual, or appropriate portions of the manual (and changes and additions) shall be made available to maintenance and ground operations personnel as well as a copy to its flight crewmembers and representatives of the administrator assigned to the certificate holder.

2. What do the regulations state concerning the preparation of load manifests? (14 CFR §135.63)

Each certificate holder is responsible for the preparation and accuracy of a load manifest in duplicate containing information concerning the loading of the aircraft. The certificate holder shall keep copies of completed load manifests for at least 30 days at its principal operations base, or at another location used by it and approved by the Administrator.

3. What are the regulations concerning reporting mechanical irregularities? (14 CFR §135.65)

a. Each certificate holder shall provide an aircraft maintenance log to be carried on board each aircraft for recording or deferring mechanical irregularities and their correction.

b. The pilot-in-command shall enter or have entered in the aircraft maintenance log each mechanical irregularity that comes to the pilot's attention during flight time. Before each flight, the pilot-in-command shall determine the status of each irregularity entered in the maintenance log at the end of the preceding flight (if such information is not already known).

c. Each person who takes corrective action or defers action concerning a reported or observed failure or malfunction, shall record the action taken in the aircraft maintenance log.

d. Copies of the aircraft maintenance log will be maintained in the aircraft for access by appropriate personnel.

4. Which persons may be carried aboard an aircraft without complying with the passenger carrying requirements of 14 CFR Part 135? (14 CFR §135.85)

a. A crewmember or other employee of the certificate holder.

b. A person necessary for the safe handling of animals on the aircraft.

c. A person necessary for the safe handling of hazardous materials.

d. A person performing duty as a security or honor guard accompanying a shipment made by or under the authority of the U.S. government.

Continued

e. A military courier or a military route supervisor carried by a
military cargo contract air carrier or commercial operator in
operations under a military cargo contract, if that carriage is
specifically authorized by the appropriate military service.

f. An authorized representative of the Administrator conducting
an enroute inspection.

g. A person, authorized by the Administrator, who is performing a
duty connected with a cargo operation of the certificate holder.

h. A DOD commercial air carrier evaluator conducting an en route
evaluation.

5. What are the regulations concerning carriage of cargo (including carry-on baggage) in or on the aircraft? (14 CFR §135.87)

No person may carry cargo, including carry-on baggage, in or on
any aircraft unless it is carried in an approved cargo rack, bin, or
compartment installed in or on the aircraft and it is secured by an
approved means.

6. What are the pilot oxygen requirements? (14 CFR §135.89)

Unpressurized aircraft. At altitudes above 10,000 feet through
12,000 feet MSL for that part of the flight at those altitudes that
is of more than 30 minutes duration and at altitudes above 12,000
feet MSL, each pilot must use oxygen continuously.

Pressurized aircraft. Use of supplemental oxygen as follows:

• Above 12,000 feet cabin pressure altitude—pilot at controls
must use oxygen continuously.

• Above FL250—if one pilot leaves duty station, remaining pilot
shall use oxygen.

• Through FL350—maximum altitude without one pilot wearing
and using oxygen mask (if quick-donning oxygen mask
available).

• Above FL350—at least one pilot shall wear a secured and
sealed oxygen mask (quick-donning type).

7. **What is the minimum passenger-seating configuration that requires a second-in-command?** (14 CFR §135.99)

If the aircraft has a passenger-seating configuration of 10 seats or more (excluding any pilot seat), a second-in-command is required.

8. **What passenger-seating configuration (excluding any pilot seat) requires a flight attendant crewmember to be on board?** (14 CFR §135.107)

No certificate holder may operate an aircraft that has a passenger-seating configuration of more than 19 (excluding any pilot seat), unless there is a flight attendant crewmember on board the aircraft.

9. **Before each takeoff, the pilot-in-command of an aircraft carrying passengers shall ensure that all passengers have been orally briefed on what information?** (14 CFR §135.117)

The pilot-in-command shall ensure that all have been orally briefed on smoking, the use of safety belts, the placement of seat backs in an upright position before takeoff and landing, location and means for opening the passenger entry door and emergency exits, location of survival equipment, ditching procedures and the use of required flotation equipment (if the flight involves extended overwater operation), the normal and emergency use of oxygen (if the flight involves operations above 12,000 feet MSL), and the location and operation of fire extinguishers.

10. **What aircraft, operating under 14 CFR Part 135, are required to have a third gyroscopic bank and pitch indicator installed?** (14 CFR §135.149)

Turbojet airplanes—in addition to two gyroscopic bank and pitch indicators (artificial horizons) for use at the pilot stations, a third indicator must also be installed.

11. Which aircraft must be equipped with an approved public address and crewmember interphone system? (14 CFR §135.150)

No person may operate an aircraft having a passenger-seating configuration of more than 19 (excluding any pilot seat), unless it is equipped with a public address system and a crewmember interphone system.

12. What aircraft are required to have an approved cockpit voice recorder on board? (14 CFR §135.151)

A multiengine, turbine-powered airplane or rotorcraft having a passenger seating configuration of six or more and for which two pilots are required by certification or operating rules or that has a passenger seating configuration of 20 or more.

13. What are the passenger oxygen requirements? (14 CFR §135.157)

Unpressurized aircraft—above 15,000 feet MSL, all passengers must be supplied with oxygen. Above 10,000 feet through 15,000 feet MSL, 10 percent of passengers must be supplied with oxygen for any part of flight of more than 30 minutes at those altitudes.

Pressurized aircraft—above 15,000 feet MSL, the oxygen requirement depends on the aircraft's ability to descend safely to an altitude of 15,000 feet MSL in 4 minutes. If the aircraft can safely descend to 15,000 feet MSL within four minutes, only a 30-minute supply is required.

14. What is the required emergency equipment for extended overwater operations? (14 CFR §135.167)

For extended overwater operations (greater than 50 NM from nearest shoreline)—each seated occupant (not just passengers) must have:

a. Life preservers within easy reach and with approved survivor locator light.

b. Enough approved life rafts (to accommodate the occupants of the aircraft) which will include at least one approved survivor locator light, one approved pyrotechnic signaling device and additional equipment as specified in 14 CFR §135.167.

c. One raft must have a survival-type emergency locator transmitter.

15. In which aircraft, or under what conditions, is airborne thunderstorm detection equipment required? (14 CFR §135.173)

No person may operate an aircraft that has a passenger-seating configuration, of 10 seats or more (excluding any pilot seat) in passenger carrying operations, except a helicopter operating under day VFR conditions, unless the aircraft is equipped with either approved thunderstorm detection equipment or approved airborne weather radar equipment.

16. What are the emergency equipment requirements for aircraft having a passenger-seating configuration of more than 19 passengers? (14 CFR §135.177)

No person may operate an aircraft having a passenger-seating configuration of more than 19 seats (excluding any pilot seat), unless it is equipped with the following emergency equipment:

a. One approved first aid kit for treatment of injuries likely to occur in flight or in a minor accident.

b. A crash ax carried so as to be accessible to the crew but inaccessible to passengers during normal operations.

c. Signs that are visible to all occupants to notify them when smoking is prohibited and when safety belts must be fastened.

17. To operate an aircraft with certain equipment inoperative under the provisions of a minimum equipment list, what document authorizing it must be issued to the certificate holder? (14 CFR §135.179)

No person may takeoff an aircraft with inoperable instruments or equipment installed unless an approved Minimum Equipment List (MEL) exists for that aircraft and the certificate-holding district office has issued the certificate holder operations specifications authorizing operations in accordance with an approved Minimum Equipment List.

18. **A takeoff may not be made from an airport that is below the authorized IFR landing minimums unless what conditions are met?** (14 CFR §135.217)

There must be an alternate airport with the required IFR landing minimums within 1 hour flying time, at normal cruising speed in still air.

19. **What weather must be forecast to exist at ETA for the destination airport, before a pilot may begin an IFR operation to that airport?** (14 CFR §135.219)

No person may takeoff an aircraft under IFR or begin an IFR or over the top operation unless the latest weather reports or forecasts, or any combination of them, indicate that weather conditions at the estimated time of arrival at the next airport of intended landing will be at or above authorized IFR landing minimums.

20. **When is an alternate for a destination airport not required for a Part 135 flight operating in IFR conditions?** (14 CFR §135.223)

No alternate airport is required if a standard instrument approach procedure for the first airport of intended landing is provided and, for at least one hour before and after the estimated time of arrival, the appropriate weather reports or forecasts, or any combination of them, indicate that:

a. The ceiling will be at least 1,500 feet above the lowest circling approach MDA; or

b. If a circling instrument approach is not authorized for the airport, the ceiling will be at least 1,500 feet above the lowest published minimum or 2,000 feet above the airport elevation, whichever is higher; and

c. Visibility for that airport is forecast to be at least three miles, or two miles more than the lowest applicable visibility minimums, whichever is the greater, for the instrument approach procedure to be used at the destination airport.

21. **An instrument approach procedure to an airport may not be initiated unless the latest weather report indicates what weather conditions?** (14 CFR §135.225)

The weather report issued by the weather reporting facility at that airport must indicate that weather conditions are at or above the authorized IFR landing minimums for that airport.

22. **After passing the final approach fix on a VOR approach, a weather report is received indicating the visibility is below prescribed minimums. What action should be taken?** (14 CFR §135.225)

The pilot may continue the approach and land if, at the MDA, the pilot finds that the actual weather conditions are at least equal to the minimums prescribed for the procedure.

23. **What are the operational requirements concerning frost, ice and snow on aircraft surfaces during takeoff?** (14 CFR 135.227)

Except under certain conditions, no pilot may takeoff an aircraft that has frost, ice, or snow adhering to any rotor blade, propeller, windshield, stabilizing or control surface, to a powerplant installation, or to an airspeed, altimeter, rate-of-climb, flight attitude instrument system or wing.

24. **To act as pilot-in-command of an aircraft during IFR operations under Part 135, what minimum experience is required?** (14 CFR §135.243)

The pilot-in-command must hold at least a Commercial Pilot Certificate with appropriate category and class ratings and if required, an appropriate type rating for that aircraft; also 1,200 hours flight time as a pilot including:

a. 500 hours of cross-country flight time;

b. 100 hours of night time; and

c. 75 hours of actual or simulated instrument time, at least 50 hours of which were in actual flight.

d. Holds an instrument rating or an airline transport pilot certificate with an airplane category rating.

25. What are the operating experience requirements that must be met before a pilot may act as PIC of an aircraft operated by a commuter air carrier in passenger-carrying operations? (14 CFR §135.244)

The pilot-in-command must have completed the following operating experience in each make and basic model of aircraft to be flown:

- Single engine — 10 hours.
- Multi-engine, reciprocating — 15 hours.
- Multi-engine, turbine-powered — 20 hours.
- Turbojet-powered — 25 hours.

Note: Hours of operating experience may be reduced to not less than 50 percent of hours required by the substitution of one additional takeoff and landing for each hour of flight.

26. What are the flight time limitation and rest requirements for Part 135 scheduled operations? (14 CFR §135.265)

No certificate holder may schedule any flight crewmember, and no flight crewmember may accept an assignment, for flight time in scheduled operations or in other commercial flying if that crewmember's total flight time in all commercial flying will exceed:

a. 1,200 hours in any calendar year.

b. 120 hours in any calendar month.

c. 34 hours in any 7 consecutive days.

d. 8 hours during any 24 consecutive hours for a flight crew consisting of one pilot.

e. 8 hours between required rest periods for a flight crew consisting of two pilots qualified under Part 135 for the operation being conducted.

27. What are the instrument proficiency check requirements to act as pilot-in-command under IFR? (14 CFR §135.297)

No certificate holder may use a pilot, nor may any person serve as a pilot-in-command of an aircraft under IFR unless, since the beginning of the 6th calendar month before that service, that pilot has passed an instrument proficiency check under this section administered by the Administrator or an authorized check pilot.

28. **To serve as pilot-in-command in a Part 135 IFR operation, a person must have passed a line check. How often are these required?** (14 CFR §135.299)

No certificate holder may use a pilot, nor may any person serve as a pilot-in-command of a flight unless, since the beginning of the 12th calendar month before that service, that pilot has passed a flight check in one of the types of aircraft which that pilot is to fly.

29. **What type of emergency training must a certificate holder provide to flight crews operating above FL250?** (14 CFR §135.331)

Emergency training in such subjects as:

a. Respiration

b. Hypoxia

c. Duration of consciousness without supplemental oxygen at altitudes

d. Gas expansion

e. Gas bubble formation

f. Physical phenomena and incidents of decompression

30. **What are the training requirements for persons involved in the handling or carriage of hazardous materials?** (14 CFR §135.505)

No certificate holder may use any crewmember or person to perform any of the job functions or direct supervisory responsibilities, and no person may perform any of the job functions or direct supervisory responsibilities, unless that person has satisfactorily completed the certificate holder's FAA-approved initial or recurrent hazardous materials training program within the past 24 months.

31. **What is Part 125?** (AC 125-1)

The 14 CFR Part 125 regulations were issued to establish a uniform set of certification and operational rules for large airplanes having a seating capacity of 20 or more passengers, or a maximum payload capacity of 6,000 pounds or more, when used for private carriage. These rules substantially upgrade the level of safety applicable to large airplanes formerly operated under Part 91.

Instrument
Procedures

6

A. Departure

1. What are "gate hold" procedures? (P/CG)

Procedures at selected airports to hold aircraft at the gate or other ground location whenever departure delays exceed or are anticipated to exceed 15 minutes. Pilots should monitor ground control/clearance delivery frequency for engine start/taxi advisories or new proposed start/taxi time if the delay changes.

2. What are pre-taxi clearance procedures? (AIM 5-2-1)

Certain airports have established pre-taxi clearance programs whereby pilots of departing IFR aircraft may elect to receive their IFR clearances before they start taxiing for takeoff. Pilot participation is not mandatory. Participating pilots should call clearance delivery or ground control not more than 10 minutes before proposed taxi time, and once clearance is received, call ground control when ready to taxi.

3. What clearance items are given in an abbreviated IFR clearance? (AIM 5-2-5)

C learance Limit (destination airport or fix)
R oute (initial heading)
A ltitude (initial altitude)
F requency (departure)
T ransponder (squawk code)

4. What does "clearance void time" mean? (P/CG)

Used by ATC to advise an aircraft that the departure clearance is automatically cancelled if takeoff is not made prior to the specified time. The pilot must obtain a new clearance or cancel his/her IFR flight plan if not off by the specified time. Usually received when conducting operations from airports without a tower.

5. **What is the purpose of the term "hold for release" when included in an IFR clearance?** (AIM 5-2-6)

ATC may issue "hold for release" instructions in a clearance to delay an aircraft's departure for traffic management reasons (weather, traffic volume, etc.). A pilot may not depart utilizing that IFR clearance until a release time or additional instructions are received from ATC.

6. **What is the pilot's responsibility for readback of a clearance instruction?** (AIM 4-4-7)

Pilots of airborne aircraft should read back those parts of ATC clearances and instructions containing altitude assignments or vectors as a means of mutual verification. Include the aircraft identification in all readbacks and acknowledgments. Readback altitudes, altitude restrictions, and vectors in the same sequence as they are given in the clearance or instruction.

7. **What are DPs, and why are they necessary?** (AIM 5-2-8)

Departure procedures are pre-planned IFR procedures that provide obstruction clearance from the terminal area to the enroute structure. At busier airports, they also increase efficiency and reduce communications and departure delays through the use of SIDs. There are two types of DPs—Obstacle Departure Procedures (ODPs), and Standard Instrument Departures (SIDs).

8. **What minimums are necessary for IFR takeoff under 14 CFR Parts 121, 125, 129 and 135?** (14 CFR §91.175)

For aircraft operated under Parts 121, 125, 129 or 135, if takeoff minimums are not prescribed under Part 97 for a particular airport, the following minimums apply to takeoffs under IFR for aircraft operating under those parts:

For 2 engines or less .... 1 SM visibility
For more than 2 engines.................. $1/2$ SM visibility

B. En Route

1. What are "jet routes"? (AIM 5-3-4)

Turbine-powered aircraft spend most of their time operating on jet routes. The jet route system consists of routes established from 18,000 feet MSL to FL450 inclusive. These routes are depicted on Enroute High Altitude Charts. Jet routes are depicted in black on aeronautical charts and are identified by a "J" (Jet) followed by the airway number (e.g., J12). Jet routes, as VOR airways, are predicated solely on VOR or VORTAC navigation facilities (except in Alaska).

2. What is a VOR changeover point (COP)? (AIM 5-3-6)

The COP is a point along the route or airway segment between two adjacent navigation facilities or waypoints where changeover in navigation guidance should occur. COPs are established for the purpose of preventing loss of navigation guidance, to prevent frequency interference from other facilities, and to prevent use of different facilities by different aircraft in the same airspace.

3. Describe the climb procedure when approaching a fix beyond which a higher MEA exists. (FAA-H-8083-15)

When an MEA, MOCA, and/or MAA change on a segment other than a NAVAID, a sideways "T" is depicted on the chart. If there is an airway break without the symbol, you can assume the altitudes have not changed. When a change of MEA to a higher MEA is required, the climb may commence at the break, ensuring obstacle clearance.

4. Describe the climb procedure when approaching a fix at which a MCA exists. (FAA-H-8083-15)

A MCA will be charted when a higher MEA route segment is approached. The MCA is usually indicated when you are approaching steeply rising terrain, and obstacle clearance and/or signal reception is compromised. In this case, the pilot is required to initiate a climb so the MCA is reached by the time the intersection is crossed.

5. Define the following. (P/CG)

MEA—Minimum enroute altitude; the lowest published altitude between radio fixes that ensures acceptable navigational signal coverage and meets obstacle clearance requirements.

MOCA—Minimum obstacle clearance altitude; the lowest published altitude between radio fixes that meets obstacle clearance requirements. It also ensures acceptable navigational signal coverage within 22 NM of a VOR.

MCA—Minimum crossing altitude; the lowest altitude at certain fixes at which aircraft must cross when proceeding in the direction of a higher MEA.

MRA—Minimum reception altitude; the lowest altitude at which an intersection can be determined.

MAA—Maximum authorized altitude; the highest altitude on a Federal airway, jet route, RNAV low or high route, or other direct route for which an MEA is designated at which adequate reception of navigation aid signals is assured.

OROCA—Off route obstruction clearance altitude; provides obstruction clearance with a 1,000-foot buffer in non-mountainous terrain areas and a 2,000-foot buffer in designated mountainous areas within the United States. This altitude may not provide signal or communication coverage from ground-based navigational aids or ATC radar.

6. If no applicable minimum altitude is prescribed (no MEA or MOCA), what minimum altitudes apply for IFR operations? (14 CFR §91.177)

Minimum altitudes are:

a. Mountainous terrain (designated in 14 CFR Part 95)—at least an altitude of 2,000 feet above the highest obstacle within a horizontal distance of 4 NM from the course to be flown.

b. Other than mountainous terrain—at least 1,000 feet above the highest obstacle within a horizontal distance of 4 NM from the course to be flown.

7. **What reports should be made to ATC at all times without a specific request?** (AIM 5-3-3)

The pilot must report:

a. When vacating any previously assigned altitude or flight level for a newly assigned altitude or flight level.

b. When an altitude change will be made if operating on a clearance specifying VFR-On-Top.

c. When unable to climb/descend at a rate of at least 500 feet per minute.

d. When approach has been missed (request clearance for specific action, i.e., to alternate airport, another approach, etc.).

e. Change in the average true speed (at cruising altitude) when it varies by 5 percent or 10 knots (whichever is greater) from that filed in the flight plan.

f. The time and altitude or flight level upon reaching a holding fix or point that the pilot is cleared to.

g. When leaving any assigned holding fix or point.

h. In controlled airspace, any loss of VOR, TACAN, ADF, low frequency navigation receiver capability, IFR approved GPS/GNSS receiver anomalies, complete or partial loss of ILS receiver capability or impairment of air/ground communications capability.

i. Any information relating to the safety of flight.

j. Upon encountering weather or hazardous conditions not forecast.

8. **What reporting requirements are required by ATC when not in radar contact?** (AIM 5-3-3)

a. When leaving final approach fix inbound on the final approach (nonprecision approach) or when leaving the outer marker (or fix used in lieu of the outer marker) inbound on final (precision) approach.

b. A corrected estimate at anytime it becomes apparent that an estimate, as previously submitted, is in error in excess of 3 minutes.

9. **What items of information should be included in every position report?** (AIM 5-3-2)

   a. Identification

   b. Position

   c. Time

   d. Altitude or flight level

   e. Type of flight plan (not required in IFR position reports made directly to ARTCCs or approach control)

   f. ETA and name of next reporting point

   g. The name only of the next succeeding reporting point along the route of flight

   h. Pertinent remarks

10. **Explain the terms "maintain" and "cruise" as they pertain to an IFR altitude assignment.** (AIM 4-4-3)

    Maintain—(Self-explanatory) maintain last altitude assigned.

    Cruise—Used instead of "maintain" to assign a block of airspace to a pilot, from minimum IFR altitude up to and including the altitude specified in the cruise clearance. The pilot may level off at any intermediate altitude, and climb/descent may be made at the discretion of the pilot. However, once the pilot starts a descent, and *verbally* reports leaving an altitude in the block, he may not return to that altitude without additional ATC clearance.

11. **Can an ATC "cruise" clearance also authorize you to execute an approach at the destination airport?** (FAA-H-8261-1)

    Yes; ATC may issue a cruise clearance that authorizes you to execute an approach upon arrival at the destination airport, and will not issue further clearance for approach and landing. When operating in uncontrolled airspace on a cruise clearance, you are responsible for determining the minimum IFR altitude. Descent and landing at an airport in uncontrolled airspace are governed by the applicable visual flight rules and/or operations specifications.

12. Concerning two-way radio communications failure in VFR and IFR conditions, what is the procedure for altitude, route, leaving holding fix, descent for approach, and approach selection? (14 CFR §91.185)

VFR conditions: If the failure occurs in VFR conditions, or if VFR conditions are encountered after the failure, each pilot shall continue the flight under VFR and land as soon as practicable.

IFR conditions: If the failure occurs in IFR conditions, or if the above (*VFR conditions*) cannot be complied with, each pilot shall continue the flight according to the following:

a. Route.

   i. By the route assigned in the last ATC clearance received;

   ii. If being radar vectored, by the direct route from the point of radio failure to the fix, route, or airway specified in the vector clearance;

   iii. With no assigned route, by the route that ATC has advised may be expected in a further clearance; or

   iv. With no assigned route or a route that ATC has advised may be expected in a further clearance, by the route filed in the flight plan.

b. Altitude. At the highest of the following altitudes or flight levels for the route segment being flown:

   i. The altitude or flight level assigned in the last ATC clearance received;

   ii. The minimum altitude (converted, if appropriate, to minimum flight level as prescribed in §91.121(c)) for IFR operations; or

   iii. The altitude or flight level ATC has advised may be expected in a further clearance.

c. Leave clearance limit.

   i. When the clearance limit is a fix from which an approach begins, commence descent, or descent and approach, as close as possible to the expect-further-clearance (EFC) time

Continued

if one has been received. If one has not been received, as close as possible to the ETA as calculated from the filed or amended (with ATC) estimated time en route (ETE).

ii. If the clearance limit is not a fix from which an approach begins, leave the clearance limit at the EFC time. However, if an EFC has not been received, leave the fix at a point upon arrival over the clearance limit. Then proceed to a fix from which an approach begins, and commence descent or descent and approach as close as possible to the ETA as calculated from the filed or amended ETE.

13. What are RNAV routes and the requirements to use them? (AIM 5-3-4)

Published RNAV routes, including Q-Routes and T-Routes, can be flight-planned for use by aircraft with RNAV capability, subject to limitations or requirements noted on enroute charts, in applicable Advisory Circulars, or by NOTAM. Depicted in blue on charts and identified by the letter "Q" or "T" followed by the airway number (e.g. Q-13, T-205).

14. What is the main difference between a "Q" route and a "T" route? (AIM 5-3-4)

a. *Q-routes* — are for use by RNAV-equipped aircraft between 18,000 feet MSL and FL 450 inclusive.

b. *T-routes* — are for use by RNAV-equipped aircraft from 1,200 feet above the surface (or in some instances higher), up to but not including 18,000 feet MSL.

15. What are "unpublished" RNAV routes and the requirements to fly them? (AIM 5-3-4)

Unpublished RNAV routes are direct routes, based on area navigation capability, between waypoints defined in terms of latitude/longitude coordinates, degree-distance fixes, or offsets from established routes/airways at a specified distance and direction. Radar monitoring by ATC is required on all unpublished RNAV routes.

C. Arrival

1. What is a STAR? (AIM 5-4-1)

A *standard terminal arrival route* is an ATC coded IFR arrival route established for use by arriving IFR aircraft destined for certain airports. RNAV STAR/FMSP procedures for arrivals serve the same purpose but are only used by aircraft equipped with FMS or GPS. The purpose of both is to simplify clearance delivery procedures and facilitate transition between en route and instrument approach procedures. Reference the *Terminal Procedures Publication* (TPP) for the availability of STARs.

2. When being radar-vectored for an approach, at what point may you start a descent from your last assigned altitude to a lower altitude if "cleared for the approach"? (AIM 5-5-4)

When "cleared for the approach" the pilot may begin descent from last assigned altitude when established on a segment of a published route or instrument approach procedure.

3. What is a profile descent? (P/CG)

A profile descent is an uninterrupted descent (except where level flight is required for speed adjustment; e.g., 250 knots at 10,000 feet MSL) from cruising altitude/level to interception of a glide slope or to a minimum altitude specified for the initial or intermediate approach segment of a nonprecision instrument approach. The profile descent normally terminates at the approach gate or where the glide slope or other appropriate minimum altitude is intercepted.

4. What is a minimum vectoring altitude (MVA)? (P/CG and AIM 5-4-5)

MVA is the lowest MSL altitude at which an IFR aircraft will be vectored by a radar controller, except as otherwise authorized for radar approaches, departures, and missed approaches. The altitude meets IFR obstacle clearance criteria. It may be lower than the published MEA along an airway or J-route segment. It may be used for radar vectoring only upon the controller's determination that an adequate radar return is being received from the aircraft being controlled. Charts depicting minimum vectoring altitudes are normally available only to the controllers and not to the pilots.

5. What is a minimum sector altitude (MSA) and what does it guarantee? (P/CG)

These are altitudes depicted on approach charts that provide at least 1,000 feet of obstacle clearance within a 25-mile radius of the navigation facility upon which the procedure is predicated. Sectors depicted on approach charts must be at least 90 degrees in scope. These altitudes are for emergency use only and do not necessarily ensure acceptable navigational signal coverage.

6. What procedure is to be used when the clearance "cleared for the visual" is issued? (AIM 5-4-22)

A visual approach is conducted on an IFR flight plan and authorizes a pilot to proceed visually and clear of clouds to the airport. The pilot must have either the airport or the preceding identified aircraft in sight. This approach must be authorized and controlled by the appropriate ATC facility. Reported weather at the airport must have a ceiling at or above 1,000 feet and visibility 3 miles or greater. Visual approaches are IFR procedures conducted under IFR in visual meteorological conditions. Cloud clearance requirements of 14 CFR §91.155 are not applicable.

7. Describe the term "contact approach." (P/CG)

An approach in which an aircraft on an IFR flight plan, having an ATC authorization, operating clear of clouds with at least 1 mile flight visibility and a reasonable expectation of continuing to the destination airport in those conditions, may deviate from the instrument approach procedure and proceed to the destination airport by visual reference to the surface. This approach will only be authorized when requested by the pilot and the reported ground visibility at the destination airport is at least 1 statute mile.

8. When is a procedure turn not required? (AIM 5-4-9)

A procedure turn is not required when:

a. The symbol "NoPT" is depicted.

b. "Radar Vectoring" is provided.

c. A holding pattern is published in lieu of a procedure turn.

d. Conducting a timed approach.

e. The procedure turn is not authorized (absence of procedure turn barb on plan view).

9. What are standard procedure turn limitations?
(AIM 5-4-9)

a. Turn on the depicted side.

b. Adhere to depicted minimum altitudes.

c. Complete the maneuver within the distance specified in the profile view.

d. Maneuver at a maximum speed not greater than 200 knots (IAS).

D. Holding

1. What information will ATC provide when they request a hold at a fix where the holding pattern is not charted?
(AIM 5-3-7)

An ATC clearance requiring an aircraft to hold at a fix where the pattern is not charted will include the following information:

a. Direction of holding from the fix in terms of eight cardinal compass points.

b. Holding fix (may be omitted if included at the beginning of the transmission as the clearance limit).

c. Radial, course, bearing, airway or route on which the aircraft is to hold.

d. Leg length in miles if DME or RNAV is to be used (leg length will be specified in minutes on pilot request or if the controller considers it necessary).

Continued

e. Direction of turn if left turns are to be made, the pilot requests, or the controller considers it necessary.

f. Time to expect further clearance and any pertinent additional delay information.

2. What is the maximum speed permitted for aircraft while holding? (AIM 5-3-7)

MHA–6,000 ft.................................. 200 KIAS

6,001–14,000 ft............................... 230 KIAS

14,001–and above .... 265 KIAS

Note: Holding patterns may be restricted to a maximum speed depicted in parentheses inside the holding pattern on the chart: e.g., (175). Holding patterns from 6,001' to 14,000' may be restricted to a maximum airspeed of 210 KIAS. These nonstandard patterns will be depicted by an icon.

3. What action is appropriate when approaching a holding fix at an airspeed in excess of maximum holding speed? (AIM 5-3-7)

Start a speed reduction when 3 minutes or less from the fix. Speed may be reduced earlier, but ATC must be advised of the change.

4. What is the leg length for a standard holding pattern? (AIM 5-3-7)

The standard leg length is:

a. 1 minute inbound at or below 14,000 feet MSL, and

b. $1^1/_2$ minutes inbound above 14,000 feet MSL.

E. Precision Instrument Approaches

1. Define a precision approach. (P/CG)

A precision approach is a standard instrument approach procedure in which an electronic glide slope/glide path is provided. Examples are: ILS, MLS, and PAR.

2. What are the basic components of a standard ILS? (AIM 1-1-9)

Guidance... Localizer, glide slope

Range .... Marker beacons, DME

Visual.. Approach lights, touchdown and centerline lights, runway lights

3. Describe both visual and aural indications a pilot would receive when crossing the outer, middle, and inner markers of a standard ILS. (AIM 1-1-9)

Outer Marker	Middle Marker	Inner Marker
blue light	amber light	white light
dull tone	medium tone	high tone
slow speed	medium speed	high speed
– – – – – –	– . – . –	.. . . . .

4. What are the distances from the landing threshold of the outer, middle, and inner markers? (AIM 1-1-9, P/CG)

Outer marker.................................... 4 to 7 miles from threshold

Middle marker .... 3,500 feet from threshold

Inner marker.................................... between middle marker and threshold

5. When is the inner marker used? (AIM 1-1-9)

Ordinarily, there are two marker beacons associated with an ILS, the outer marker (OM) and middle marker (MM). Locations with a Category II and III ILS also have an inner marker (IM). For Category II approaches, it is on at the decision height of 100 feet on the glide slope.

6. Localizers operate within what frequency range? (AIM 1-1-9)

Localizers operate on odd tenths within the 108.10 to 111.95 MHz band.

7. Where is the localizer/transmitter antenna installation located in relation to the runway? (AIM 1-1-9)

The antenna is located at the far end of the approach runway.

8. Where is the glideslope antenna located and what is its normal usable range? (AIM 1-1-9)

The glideslope transmitter is located between 750 feet and 1,250 feet from the approach end of the runway (down the runway), and offset 250 feet to 650 feet from it; normally usable to a distance of 10 NM.

9. What range does a standard localizer have? (AIM 1-1-9)

The localizer signal provides course guidance throughout the descent path to the runway threshold from a distance of 18 NM from the antenna site.

10. What is the angular width of a localizer signal? (AIM 1-1-9)

The localizer signal is adjusted to provide an angular width of between 3° to 6°, as necessary to provide a linear width of 700 feet at the runway approach threshold.

11. What is the normal glide slope angle for a standard ILS? (AIM 1-1-9)

The standard glide slope angle for an ILS is 3° with a depth of 1.4°.

12. What two methods can be used to obtain the rate of descent required to maintain a 3° ILS glide slope? Ground speed is 120 knots.

a. Ground speed (120) × 5 = 600. 600 fpm is the approximate rate of descent required to maintain a 3° glide slope.

b. Ground speed (120) ÷ 2 = 60; add a zero to the result, to get 600. 600 fpm is the approximate rate of descent required to maintain a 3° glide slope.

13. What is the sensitivity of a CDI tuned to a localizer signal compared with a CDI tuned to a VOR? (FAA-H-8083-15)

Full left or full right deflection occurs at approximately 2.5° from the centerline of a localizer course, which is 4 times greater than when tuned to a VOR where full-scale deflection equals 10° from the centerline.

14. Define the term "decision height" (DH). (14 CFR Part 1)

Decision height (DH) is a specified height above the ground in an instrument approach procedure at which the pilot must decide whether to initiate an immediate missed approach if the pilot does not see the required visual reference, or to continue the approach. DH is expressed in feet above ground level.

15. When flying an instrument approach procedure, when can the pilot descend below the MDA or DH? (14 CFR §91.175)

No person may operate an aircraft below the prescribed MDA or continue an approach below the authorized DH unless:

a. The aircraft is continuously in a position from which a descent to a landing on the intended runway can be made at a normal rate of descent using normal maneuvers; additionally, for Part 121 and 135 operations, unless that descent rate will allow touchdown to occur within the touchdown zone of the runway of intended landing.

b. The flight visibility is not less than the visibility prescribed in the standard instrument approach procedure being used.

c. When at least one of the following visual references for the intended runway is distinctly visible and identifiable to the pilot—

　i. The approach light system (except that the pilot may not descend below 100 feet above the touchdown zone elevation using the ALS as a reference unless the red terminating bars or the red side row bars are also distinctly visible and identifiable).

　ii. The threshold.

Continued

    iii. The threshold markings.

    iv. The threshold lights.

    v. REIL.

    vi. VASI.

    vii. The touchdown zone markings.

    viii. The touchdown zone lights.

    ix. The runway and runway markings.

    x. The runway lights.

16. What are the legal substitutions for an inoperative outer marker? (14 CFR §91.175)

Compass locator, PAR, ASR, DME, VOR, or NDB fixes authorized in the instrument approach procedure; or a suitable RNAV system in conjunction with a fix identified in the standard instrument approach procedure.

17. What are the lowest authorized ILS Category I, II, and III minimums with all required ground and airborne systems components operative? (AIM 1-1-9)

Category I: DH 200 feet and RVR 2,400 feet (with touchdown zone and centerline lighting, RVR 1,800 feet)

Category II: DH 100 feet and RVR 1,200 feet.

Category IIIa: No DH or DH below 100 feet and RVR not less than 700 feet.

Category IIIb: No DH or with a DH below 50 feet and RVR less than 700 feet, but not less than 150 feet.

Category IIIc: No DH and no RVR limitation.

18. What are simultaneous ILS approaches? (P/CG)

An approach system permitting simultaneous ILS/MLS approaches to airports having parallel runways separated by at least 4,300 feet between centerlines. Integral parts of a total system are ILS/MLS, radar, communications, ATC procedures, and appropriate airborne equipment.

19. Convert the following RVR values to ground visibility values: 1600, 2400, 3200, 4000, 4500, 5000, 6000. (AIM 5-4-20)

1,600	1/4
2,400	1/2
3,200	5/8
4,000	3/4
4,500	7/8
5,000	1
6,000	1-1/4

F. Nonprecision Instrument Approaches

1. What is a nonprecision approach? (P/CG)

It is a standard instrument approach procedure in which no glide slope is provided.

2. Name the types of nonprecision approach procedures available. (P/CG)

VOR, GPS, TACAN, NDB, LOC, ASR, LDA, and SDF.

3. Define "MDA." (14 CFR Part 1)

Minimum descent altitude—The lowest altitude specified in an instrument approach procedure, expressed in feet above mean sea level, to which descent is authorized on final approach or during circle-to-land maneuvering until the pilot sees the required visual references for the heliport or runway of intended landing.

4. Define "VDP." (P/CG, AIM 5-4-5)

Visual descent point—A defined point on the final approach course of a nonprecision straight-in approach procedure from which normal descent from the MDA to the runway touchdown point may be commenced, provided the approach threshold of that runway, or approach lights or other markings identifiable with the approach end of that runway, are clearly visible to the pilot. Pilots not equipped to receive the VDP should fly the approach procedure as though no VDP had been provided. The VDP is identified on the profile view of the approach chart by the symbol "V."

5. What formulas may be used to calculate the VDP for a nonprecision approach?

Two methods:

a. Distance VDP (miles from the runway)—take the MDA (HAT) and divide by 300. Example: MDA is 540 AGL, divided by 300, equals 1.8 miles from end of runway.

b. Timing VDP (time from runway)—take the MDA (HAT) and multiply by 10 percent. Then subtract that value from the time from FAF to MAP. Example: MDA is 540 AGL. Time from FAF to MAP is 3:00 minutes. 540 multiplied by 10 percent equals 54 seconds. Subtract 54 seconds from 3:00 minutes (FAF to MAP time) equals 2 minutes 6 seconds. VDP occurs when 2 minutes and 6 seconds has elapsed on approach.

6. Will standard instrument approach procedures always have a final approach fix (FAF)? (FAA-H-8083-15)

No, NDB and VOR approaches with the primary navigational aid on the field will not always have a designated FAF.

7. If no FAF is published, where does the final approach segment begin on a nonprecision approach? (FAA-H-8261-1)

When no FAF is designated, such as on an approach that incorporates an on-airport VOR or NDB, a final approach point is designated and is typically located where the procedure turn intersects the final approach course inbound.

8. Certain conditions are required for an instrument approach procedure to have "straight-in" minimums published. What are they? (AIM 5-4-20)

Straight-in minimums are shown on the IAP when the final approach course is within 30 degrees of the runway alignment (15 degrees for GPS IAPs), and a normal descent can be made from the IFR altitude shown on the IAP to the runway surface.

9. What is a stepdown fix? (P/CG)

A stepdown fix permits additional descent within a segment of an instrument approach procedure by identifying a point at which a controlling obstacle has been safely overflown.

10. What does a VASI system provide? (AIM 2-1-2)

Visual descent guidance during an approach to a runway; safe obstacle clearance within plus or minus 10° of extended runway centerline up to 4 NM from the runway; glidepath angles normally set at 3°, but may be as high as 4.5° at some locations.

11. What are the major differences between SDF and LDA approaches? (FAA-H-8083-15)

In an SDF approach procedure, the SDF course may or may not be aligned with the runway; usable off-course indications are limited to 35° either side of course centerline. The SDF signal emitted is fixed at either 6° or 12°.

In the LDA approach procedure, the LDA course is of comparable utility and accuracy to a standard localizer. An LDA course is usually not aligned with the runway; however, straight-in minimums may be published where the angle between the centerline and course does not exceed 30°. If the angle exceeds 30°, only circling minimums are published.

12. What is a sidestep approach? (P/CG)

Not an approach but a visual maneuver accomplished by a pilot at the completion of an instrument approach. Permits a straight-in landing on a parallel runway not more than 1,200 feet to either side of the runway to which the instrument approach was conducted.

G. RNAV (GPS) Approaches

1. Explain how WAAS enhances the Global Positioning System. (FAA-H-8083-15)

The Wide-Area Augmentation System is a satellite navigation system consisting of the equipment and software which augments the GPS. Signals from GPS satellites are monitored by a series of ground reference stations linked to the WAAS network to determine satellite clock and ephemeris corrections. Each station in the network relays the data to a wide-area master station where the correction information is computed and uplinked to a geo-stationary satellite via a ground uplink. It is then broadcast on the GPS frequency to WAAS receivers within the broadcast coverage area.

2. What does the acronym "LAAS" refer to? (FAA-H-8083-15)

Local Area Augmentation System — a ground-based augmentation system which uses a GPS reference facility located on or in the vicinity of the airport being serviced. This facility has a reference receiver that measures GPS satellite pseudo-range and timing and retransmits the signal. Aircraft landing at LAAS-equipped airports are able to conduct approaches to Category I level and above for properly equipped aircraft.

3. A "GLS" minima line may appear on some RNAV (GPS) approach charts. What does this refer to? (AIM 1-1-21, 5-4-5)

Ground Based Augmentation System, or GBAS Landing System minimums — a minima line originally published as a placeholder for future WAAS and LAAS approach minima, and marked N/A (since no minima was published). As LAAS and WAAS procedures have evolved, most RNAV (GPS) approach charts have had the GLS minima line replaced by a WAAS LPV minima. GLS minima may still appear on some older charts, but is used only as a placeholder for future LAAS approach minima.

4. What is an "APV" approach? (AIM 5-4-5)

Approach with Vertical Guidance — an instrument approach based on a navigation system that is not required to meet the precision approach standards of ICAO Annex 10 but provides course and glidepath deviation information. Baro-VNAV, LDA with glidepath, LNAV/VNAV and LPV are APV approaches. Properly certified WAAS receivers are able to fly these procedures using a WAAS electronic glide path, which eliminates the errors that can be introduced by using barometric altimetry.

5. Explain "LPV" RNAV minimums. (AIM 5-4-5)

Localizer performance with vertical guidance—LPV lines of minima take advantage of the improved accuracy of WAAS lateral and vertical guidance to provide an approach with sensitivities that are nearly identical to those of an ILS at similar distances. The approach is designed for angular guidance with increasing sensitivity as the aircraft gets closer to the runway. The LPV has vertical guidance and is flown to a DA. Aircraft with a statement in the AFM that the installed equipment supports LPV approaches can fly this minima line.

6. The acronym "LNAV/VNAV" on an approach chart identifies what type of RNAV minimums? (AIM 5-4-5)

LNAV/VNAV identifies APV minimums developed to accommodate an RNAV IAP with vertical guidance, usually provided by approach certified Baro-VNAV, but with lateral and vertical integrity limits larger than a precision approach or LPV. Since vertical guidance is provided, the minima will be published as a DA. This minima line can be flown by aircraft with a statement in the AFM that the installed equipment supports GPS approaches and has an approach-approved barometric VNAV, or if the aircraft has been demonstrated to support LNAV/VNAV approaches. This includes TSO-C146 WAAS equipment.

7. What are "LP" RNAV minimums? (AIM 5-4-5)

Localizer Performance—approaches to "LP" lines of minima take advantage of the improved accuracy of WAAS to provide approaches with lateral and angular guidance. Angular guidance does not refer to a glideslope angle, but rather to the increased lateral sensitivity as the aircraft gets closer to the runway, (similar to localizer approaches). Minimums are depicted as a MDA rather than a DA (H). "LP" minima will only be published if terrain, obstructions, or some other reason prevent publishing a vertically guided procedure. Receivers approved for "LP" minimums must have a statement in the AFM or AFMS including "LP" as one of the approved approach types.

8. What are "LNAV" RNAV minimums? (AIM 5-4-5)

Lateral Navigation—minimums are for lateral navigation only and the approach minimum altitude will be published as a MDA. LNAV minimums support the following navigation systems: WAAS, when the navigation solution will not support vertical navigation; and GPS navigation systems which are presently authorized to conduct GPS approaches.

H. Circling Approaches

1. What are circle-to-land approaches? (P/CG)

A circle-to-land approach is not technically an approach, but a maneuver initiated by a pilot to align the aircraft with the runway for landing when a straight-in landing from an instrument approach is not possible or desirable. The maneuver is made only when authorized by ATC and visual reference with the airport is established and maintained. At tower-controlled airports, this maneuver is made only after ATC authorization has been obtained and the pilot has established required visual reference to the airport.

2. Why do certain airports have only circling minimums published? (AIM 5-4-20)

When either the normal rate of descent or the runway alignment factor of 30 degrees (15 degrees for GPS IAPs) is exceeded, a straight-in minimum is not published and a circling minimum applies.

3. Can a pilot make a straight-in landing if using an approach procedure having only circling minimums? (AIM 5-4-20)

Yes; the fact that a straight-in minimum is not published does not preclude pilots from landing straight-in, if they have the active runway in sight and have sufficient time to make a normal approach to landing. Under such conditions and when ATC has cleared them for landing on that runway, pilots are not expected to circle, even though only circling minimums are published.

4. If cleared for a "straight in VOR-DME 34 approach," can a pilot circle to land, if needed? (P/CG)

Yes, a "straight-in approach" is an instrument approach wherein final approach is begun without first having executed a procedure turn. Such an approach is not necessarily completed with a straight-in landing or made to straight-in minimums.

5. When can you begin your descent to the runway during a circling approach? (14 CFR §91.175)

Three conditions are required before descent from the MDA can occur:

a. The aircraft is continuously in a position from which a descent to a landing on the intended runway can be made at a normal rate of descent using normal maneuvers.

b. The flight visibility is not less than the visibility prescribed in the standard instrument approach being used.

c. At least one of the specific runway visual references for the intended runway is distinctly visible and identifiable to the pilot.

6. While circling to land you lose visual contact with the runway environment. At the time visual contact is lost, your approximate position is a base leg at the circling MDA. What procedure should be followed? (AIM 5-4-21)

If visual reference is lost while circling to land from an instrument approach, the pilot should make an initial climbing turn toward the landing runway and continue the turn until established on the missed approach course. Since the circling maneuver may be accomplished in more than one direction, different patterns will be required to become established on the prescribed missed approach course, depending on the aircraft position at the time visual reference is lost. Adherence to the procedure will assure that an aircraft will remain within the circling and missed approach obstacle clearance areas.

7. How can a pilot determine the approach category minimums applicable to a particular aircraft?
(FAA-H-8083-15)

Minimums are specified for various aircraft speed/weight combinations. Speeds are based upon a value 1.3 times the stalling speed of the aircraft in the landing configuration (V_{S0}) at a maximum certificated gross landing weight. An aircraft can only fit into one approach category. If it is necessary to maneuver at speeds in excess of the upper limit of the speed range for each category, the minimum for the next higher approach category should be used.

I. Missed Approaches

1. When must a pilot execute a missed approach?
(AIM 5-4-21, 5-5-5)

When one of the following conditions occurs:

a. Arrival at the missed approach point and the runway environment is not yet in sight.

b. Arrival at DH on the glide slope with the runway environment not yet in sight.

c. Anytime a pilot determines a safe landing is not possible.

d. When circling-to-land visual contact is lost.

e. When instructed by ATC.

2. On a nonprecision approach procedure, how is the missed approach point (MAP) determined?
(FAA-H-8083-15)

The pilot determines the MAP by timing from FAF when the approach aid is well away from the airport, by a fix or NAVAID when the navigation facility is located on the field, or by waypoints as defined by GPS or VOR/DME RNAV.

3. Will the MAP on a nonprecision approach always occur over the runway threshold? (AIM 5-4-5)

No; the MAP may be located anywhere, from prior to the runway threshold to past the opposite end of the runway. The MAP location on a nonprecision approach is developed based on terrain, obstructions, NAVAID location, and sometimes, air traffic considerations.

4. For a nonprecision approach, how does the pilot determine the MAP? (FAA-H-8083-15)

By timing from FAF when the approach aid is away from the airport, by a fix or NAVAID when the navigation facility is located on the field, or by waypoints as defined by GPS or VOR/DME RNAV.

5. Where is the MAP on a precision approach? (FAA-H-8261-1)

During a precision or an APV approach, the MAP occurs at the DA or DH on the glide slope.

6. During the execution of an instrument approach procedure, if you determine a missed approach is necessary due to full-scale needle deflection, what action is recommended? (AIM 5-4-21)

Obstacle protection for missed approach is predicated on the missed approach being initiated at the DA/H or at the MAP and not lower than MDA. Reasonable buffers are provided for normal maneuvers but not for abnormally early turns. Therefore, when an early missed approach is executed, the pilot should, unless otherwise cleared by ATC, fly the IAP as specified on the approach chart to the MAP at or above the MDA or DA/H before executing a turning maneuver.

7. What procedures should be followed when initiating a go-around after passing the published MAP? (AIM 5-4-21)

Initiating a go-around after passing the MAP may result in total loss of obstacle clearance. Missed approach obstacle clearance is predicated on beginning the missed approach procedure at the MAP from MDA or DA and then climbing 200 feet/NM or greater. To compensate for the possibility of reduced obstacle clearance during a go-around, a pilot should apply procedures used in takeoff planning. Pilots should refer to airport obstacle and departure data prior to initiating an instrument approach procedure.

BE-1900
Systems

Appendix A

The following questions reference the Beechcraft 1900-C systems. These questions are representative of what you are required to know about your aircraft systems. Review your aircraft's AFM for answers specific to the airplane your checkride will take place in.

The blank lines can be used to document the information for aircraft you will be flying or testing in other than the BE-1900.

A. Airframe

1. Describe the airframe of the BE-1900. (AFM)

Low-wing monoplane constructed of metal with fully cantilevered wings and a T-tail empennage.

_____

_____

_____

2. What are the general dimensions of the BE-1900? (AFM)

Wingspan — 54 feet 6 inches _____

Length — 57 feet 10 inches _____

Tail height — 14 feet 11 inches _____

3. Describe the aircraft seating arrangement. (AFM)

Seating is available for 19 passengers plus crew.

_____

_____

4. Where are the baggage compartments located and what is the maximum amount of weight allowed in each? (AFM)

Nose — located in nose and accessed by opening a door on left side of fuselage; unpressurized and accommodates 150 lbs of baggage. _Forward cabin_ — located opposite forward door and aft of the crew compartment. 250-lb weight capacity. Hangar in compartment: 100 lbs.

Continued

Aft—located at the rear of the cabin; separated from passenger compartment by a solid bulkhead; 880 pounds forward of cargo net and 630 pounds between cargo net and aft bulkhead.

_____

_____

_____

_____

_____

_____

5. Where are the emergency exits? (AFM)

Three emergency exit doors are provided. One is located on the left side of the fuselage at the trailing edge of the wing. The other two are located on the right side of the fuselage at the leading and trailing edges of the wing.

_____

_____

_____

_____

B. Flight Controls

1. Describe how the ailerons, elevators and rudders are operated. (AFM)

Conventional push-pull control wheels interconnected by a T-column operate the ailerons and elevators. The rudder is operated by rudder pedals, which are interconnected by linkages below the floor. All three systems are connected to their respective control surfaces through push rod and cable-bellcrank systems.

_____

_____

_____

_____

2. What trim tabs are provided? (AFM)

Adjustable trim tabs are located on the rudder, elevator, and ailerons. Trim tab controls are located on the center pedestal. All trim tabs can be manually adjusted. The elevator trim can also be adjusted electrically by moving a thumb switch on each control wheel. An ELEV TRIM ON/OFF is located on the pedestal.

3. What is the function of the yaw damper system? (AFM)

The yaw damper senses heading changes (compass system input) and corrects, through use of a servo, by deflecting the rudder in the necessary direction and stabilizing the yaw axis of the airplane.

C. Annunciator System

1. What does the annunciator system consist of? (AFM)

a. *Warning annunciator panel*—centrally located on glareshield panel, red readout.

b. *Caution/advisory annunciator panel*—on center subpanel with yellow caution lights and green advisory lights.

c. *Two red master warning flashers*—on glareshield directly in front of each pilot.

d. *Two yellow master caution flashers*—inboard of the master caution flashers.

e. *Press-to-test switch*—to the right of warning annunciator panel.

2. If a fault occurs that requires immediate attention, what indicator lights will illuminate? (AFM)

a. Appropriate red warning flasher in the warning annunciator panel illuminates.

b. Both master warning flashers begin flashing.

c. Illuminated light in warning annunciator panel remains illuminated until fault is corrected.

d. Master warning flashers can be extinguished by pressing the face of either flasher (even if fault has not been corrected). Will illuminate again if another warning annunciator illuminates.

_____

_____

_____

_____

3. If a fault occurs that requires attention but not immediate action, what indicator lights will illuminate? (AFM)

a. Appropriate yellow caution flasher in the caution/advisory panel illuminates.

b. Both master caution flashers begin flashing.

c. Illuminated caution annunciator in the caution/advisory annunciator panel remains illuminated until fault is corrected.

d. Master caution flashers can be extinguished by pressing the face of either flasher (even if fault has not been corrected). Will illuminate again if another caution annunciator illuminates.

_____

_____

_____

_____

4. When will the annunciator panel automatically go into "dimming" mode? (AFM)

The annunciator panel will automatically activate the dimming mode when all of the following conditions are met:

a. A generator is online.

b. The overhead floodlights switch is in the OFF position.

c. The pilot flight lights switch is in the ON position.

d. The ambient flight level in the cockpit is below a preset value.

_____

_____

_____

_____

D. Flaps

1. Describe the flap system. (AFM)

A four-position single-slotted flap system is provided, two on each wing. One is located on the outboard wing panel and one is located on the center section. Each individual flap is mounted on two tracks attached to the rear wing spar. Anti-friction rollers attached to the flap roll in the slots provided in the flap tracks.

_____

_____

_____

_____

_____

2. How are the flaps operated? (AFM)

An electric motor powers a gearbox located on the forward side of the rear spar at the centerline of the aircraft. The gearbox turns four flexible driveshafts coupled to jackscrews, one of which operates each flap.

_____

_____

3. What are the different flap settings? (AFM)

Four detents: UP, TAKEOFF, APPROACH, LANDING. Intermediate flap positions not available.

4. Which generator bus provides power to the flap motor? (AFM)

The left generator bus.

5. What protection is provided in the event of a flap asymmetry? (AFM)

Power is automatically disconnected to the flap motor in the event of a malfunction that would result in any flap being three to six degrees out of phase with the other flaps.

E. Landing Gear

1. Describe the main and nose gear assemblies on this aircraft. (AFM)

The main gear consists of a conventional air-oil strut which pivots between main structural ribs on the nacelle and retracts forward into the nacelle. The nose gear consists of a conventional air-oil strut installed in the nose which pivots on two longitudinal fuselage members and retracts aft.

2. **Describe the hydraulic extension and retraction of the landing gear.** (AFM)

   Extension and retraction is accomplished by using actuators located on each gear assembly powered by the hydraulic system. The system's electric motor drives a hydraulic pump, which directs hydraulic fluid to the extension or retraction side of the hydraulic actuators. The system is pressurized to 3,000 psi.

   _____

   _____

   _____

   _____

3. **What methods are used to prevent accidental gear retraction while on the ground?** (AFM)

   a. A safety switch is located on the right main landing gear that opens a control circuit when the gear strut is compressed.

   b. A mechanical down lock hook holds the landing gear handle in the "DOWN" position. The hook automatically disengages when the airplane leaves the ground. It can be manually overridden in case of a malfunction, by pressing the red downlock release button.

   _____

   _____

   _____

   _____

   _____

4. What indicating system is used to advise the pilot of the gear position? (AFM)

Landing gear position is provided by individual green GEAR DOWN indicator lights located on the pilot's right subpanel, labeled NOSE, L and R. A red in-transit light is also provided, located inside the clear landing gear control handle.

_____

_____

_____

_____

5. What conditions will result in the gear horn sounding and the red lights in the landing gear control handle to illuminate? (AFM)

The warning horn will sound and the landing gear control handle lights will illuminate if the flap control handle is positioned up or down, to and including APPROACH and either or both power levers are retarded with the gear not down and locked. The red lights in the handle will also illuminate when the gear is in transit, the gear is unsafe (microswitches do not agree with position of gear handle), or when the power levers are below a preset N1 value with the gear up.

_____

_____

_____

_____

_____

6. How is the landing gear locked in the up position? (AFM)

Hydraulic system pressure performs the uplock function and holds the gear in the UP position.

_____

_____

7. **The upward travel of the landing gear is stopped when what condition is satisfied?** (AFM)

   When a hydraulic pressure of 2,775 psi is obtained, a pressure switch removes power to the hydraulic pump motor.

   _____

   _____

8. **What would cause the landing gear motor to cycle in flight?** (AFM)

   When hydraulic system pressure drops below 2,320 psi.

   _____

9. **How is manual extension of the gear accomplished?** (AFM)

   An alternate extension handle is provided (located on the floor to the right of the captain's seat) which uses hydraulic fluid from a secondary reservoir directed to the extend side of the hydraulic actuators. Remove the alternate extension handle from clip, and begin to pump. Continue to pump until three green "gear down" indicator lights are illuminated. This procedure requires approximately 80 strokes to extend and lock the gear. *Note:* Gear handle must be down, landing gear relay circuit breaker must be pulled, and airspeed must be less than 180 knots.

   _____

   _____

   _____

   _____

   _____

10. **How is nosewheel steering accomplished?** (AFM)

    A mechanical linkage connected to the rudder pedals is provided. The steering system is disconnected from the rudder control system when the airplane becomes airborne. A power steering system may also be installed, consisting of an electric motor that drives a hydraulic pump, a hydraulic actuator, and a servo valve assembly.

_____

_____

F. Engines

1. What type of engines are installed on the BE-1900? (AFM)

Pratt & Whitney PT6A-65B, reverse airflow, free turbine, turbo-prop engines.

_____

2. The engine contains how many drive shafts? (AFM)

Two; one compressor (gas generator) shaft and one power turbine shaft.

_____

3. How many and what type of compressor stages are used in this engine? (AFM)

Four axial-flow stages and one centrifugal-flow stage.

_____

4. What type of combustion chamber is used? (AFM)

Annular   _____

5. What types of power and compressor turbines are used on this engine? (AFM)

Power turbine—two stage axial flow reaction turbine

_____

Compressor (gas generator) turbine—single stage axial flow reaction turbine

_____

6. What is the engine shaft horsepower rating? (AFM)

1,100 SHP

7. What is the compressor (gas generator) shaft rotational speed (N1) limits for the following operating conditions: Takeoff, Maximum Continuous, Cruise Climb, Maximum Cruise and Transient? (AFM)

104% N1 (39,000 rpm)

8. What is the approximate gear reduction ratio between the power turbine and the propeller? (AFM)

17.6 to 1

9. What are some of the items located on the engine accessory gearbox? (AFM)

Starter/generator, engine oil pump, N1 tachometer generator, low- and high-pressure fuel boost pumps, fuel control unit.

10. Describe the engine lubrication system. (AFM)

An integral tank between the engine air intake and the accessory case contains oil used to cool as well as lubricate the engine. Engine oil temperature is maintained within operational limits by an engine oil radiator located inside the lower nacelle.

11. What condition will cause the L/R OIL PRESS annunciator to illuminate in flight? (AFM)

Oil pressure has dropped below 60 psi.

12. What is the function of the "auto ignition" switches? (AFM)

When selected to ON, they provide automatic ignition to prevent engine loss due to combustion failure. Normally used during takeoff and landing as well as when operating in turbulence, icing, and heavy precipitation conditions.

_____

_____

_____

_____

13. Describe the propulsion system controls for this airplane. (AFM)

Three sets of controls are provided:

a. *Power levers*—control engine power.

b. *Condition levers*—control idle cutoff function of the fuel control unit; limits idle speed to 58% N1 for low idle, or 72% for high idle. Three positions: FUEL CUTOFF, LOW IDLE and HIGH IDLE.

c. *Propeller levers*—control constant speed propellers through a primary governor.

_____

_____

_____

_____

14. Describe how the power levers operate. (AFM)

The power levers control engine power by operation of the gas generator (N1) governor in the fuel control unit. An increase in N1 rpm causes an increase in engine power.

_____

_____

_____

15. What type of engine instrumentation is provided? (AFM)

a. *ITT indicators* — indicate engine gas temperature between compressor and power turbines.

b. *Torque meters* — indicate foot-pounds of torque applied to propeller.

c. *Propeller tachometers (N2 speed)* — indicate prop rpm.

d. *Gas generator (N1) tachometers* — indicate rotational speed of compressor shaft in percent of rpm based on 37,468 rpm at 100%.

e. *Fuel flow gauges* — indicate fuel flow in pounds per hour times 100.

f. *Combination oil temperature/pressure gauges* — pressure on the right side and temperature on the left.

_____

_____

_____

_____

_____

G. Fire Detection

1. Describe the fire detection system. (AFM)

Composed of the following:

a. Two fire zone cables installed in each nacelle interconnected to form a continuous loop.

b. A single control amplifier in flight compartment on forward bulkhead.

c. A control circuit breaker placarded FIRE DET.

d. Two toggle test switches on co-pilot's inboard subpanel.

_____

_____

_____

_____

2. What is the function of the fire cable and control amplifier? (AFM)

Heat sensitive cables are looped around the engines so as to monitor the most likely areas for fires to occur. If a fire were to occur, heating of the cable causes resistance to drop. The control amplifier will sense this drop and at a preset level, illuminate the red light in FIRE PULL "T" handle.

_____

_____

_____

_____

3. How is fire extinguishing accomplished in this aircraft? (AFM)

a. Pull the FIRE PULL "T" handle for the appropriate engine which will cause the system to arm.

b. Raise the safety-wired clear plastic cover and press face of lens, which causes pyrotechnic cartridge to discharge. One pyrotechnic cartridge in each main gear wheel well.

c. When fully discharged, yellow D light will illuminate.

_____

_____

_____

4. How is the fire detection/extinguishing system tested? (AFM)

Two toggle-type test switches placarded ENG FIRE TEST— EXT TEST, one for the left system and one for the right system are provided. The switches test the circuitry of the fire extinguisher pyrotechnic cartridges. A successful test is indicated by illumination of a yellow "D" light and the illumination of a green "OK" light on each fire extinguisher switch on the glareshield.

_____

_____

_____

_____

H. Propeller

1. Describe the propeller system. (AFM)

Conventional four-blade, composite, constant-speed, full-feathering, reversing, counter-weighted, variable-pitch propeller. The propeller is mounted on the reduction gearbox output shaft. Single-action, engine-driven propeller governors use engine oil pressure to control propeller pitch and speed. Engine oil pressure moves the propeller to high rpm (low-pitch) hydraulic stop and reverse positions. Centrifugal counterweights, assisted by a feathering spring, move the propeller blades to low rpm (high-pitch) and into the feathered position.

_____

_____

_____

_____

2. Describe how the propeller levers operate. (AFM)

Movement of the propeller lever positions a pilot valve that allows oil to be directed to or from the propeller hub, which results in an increase or decrease in propeller rpm. To feather a propeller, the propeller lever lifts a pilot valve to a position causing a complete dumping of high-pressure oil. This allows counterweights and feathering spring to change prop pitch. The propeller control levers range of operation is 1,400 to 1,700 rpm.

_____

_____

_____

3. What is "propeller ground fine" position used for? (AFM)

Used to provide maximum deceleration on the ground during landing. Takes advantage of max available propeller drag.

4. What controls the propeller blade angle while on the ground and in "ground fine"? (AFM)

The condition levers.

5. How is propeller reversing accomplished? (AFM)

Lift power levers past IDLE and GND FINE position. Power levers are now controlling engine power through the reverse range.

6. What is the function of the propeller low pitch stop? (AFM)

The low pitch stop prevents the propeller from reversing in flight.

7. Describe the function of the propeller synchrophaser, synchronizer and synchroscope. (AFM)

a. *Synchrophaser*—positions propellers at a preset phase relationship which assists in decreasing cabin noise. First adjust prop levers or synchronization, then switch on.

b. *Synchronizer*—matches the rpm of the slower propeller to the faster propeller.

c. *Synchroscope*—instrument in the cockpit used to display difference in rpm between propellers. The gage consists of a small propeller that rotates in the direction of the higher rpm propeller.

8. **What are the three types of propeller governors and what is their function?** (AFM)

    a. *Primary (constant speed) governor*—mounted on the reduction gear housing, controls the propeller throughout its normal operating range. The primary governor has authority within the 1,400 to 1,700 rpm range.

    b. *Fuel topping*—prevents the power turbine from overspeeding by reducing the amount of fuel to the fuel control unit.

    c. *Overspeed governor*—in the event of a constant-speed governor malfunction (requesting more than 1,700 rpm) the overspeed governor activates at 1,768 rpm and dumps oil pressure from the propeller to keep rpm from exceeding approximately 1,768 rpm.

    _____

    _____

    _____

    _____

    _____

9. **How do the propeller governors control rpm?** (AFM)

    They utilize engine oil pressure.

10. **What happens to propeller blade angle as oil enters the propeller hub? Leaves the hub?** (AFM)

    As oil enters, it causes the propeller blade angle to decrease. As it leaves the hub, the propeller blade angle will increase.

    _____

    _____

    _____

11. **If a propeller overspeed occurs, what does this indicate?** (AFM)

    A failure of the primary governor has occurred.

    _____

12. How does the autofeather system work and when must it be armed? (AFM)

In the event of an engine failure, the autofeather system automatically dumps oil from the propeller servo, which enables the feathering spring and counterweights to start the feathering action of the blades. The autofeather system must be armed for takeoff, climb, approach and landing.

13. When does the autofeather system arm? (AFM)

a. Autofeather switch is in the ARM position.

b. Both power levers are greater than 88 to 91 percent N1.

c. Torque is greater than 525 feet-pounds.

14. With the autofeather system armed, what will happen in the event of an engine failure? (AFM)

When torque is less than 320 foot-pounds, the system will feather the propeller.

I. Fuel System

1. Describe the fuel tank system. (AFM)

a. Two integral fuel tanks in each wing.

b. Main tank extends from the nacelle to the wingtip; 241.3 gallons usable; filled from a port located near wing tip.

c. Collector tank (located inside each main tank) is supplied fuel from the main tank by gravity feed and two jet transfer pumps. Ensures a constant fuel level in collector tank at normal flight attitudes.

d. Auxiliary tank is located between fuselage and nacelle; 92.3 gallons usable; filled from a port located inboard of nacelle.

_____

_____

_____

_____

_____

2. What are the different types of fuel pumps? (AFM)

a. *Engine-driven fuel pump* — high-pressure, mounted on accessory case along with fuel control unit.

b. *Engine-driven primary boost pump* — low-pressure, mounted on drive pad at aft accessory section.

c. *Electrically-driven standby pump* — low pressure, located in bottom of collector tank sump. Serves as backup for engine driven pump; also provides cross-transfer fuel flow.

d. *Electrically-driven auxiliary fuel pumps* — transfer fuel to the collector tank in same wing.

_____

_____

_____

_____

_____

3. What will happen in the event of an engine-driven pump failure? (AFM)

Failure of the engine-driven, high-pressure fuel pump will result in an immediate engine flame-out.

_____

_____

4. Where are the fuel drains located? (AFM)

Six drains in each wing:

- One drain for auxiliary tank located underside of wing inboard of nacelle.
- Two drains for collector tank located outboard side of nacelle.
- Two drains for main tank located underside of wing, outboard of nacelle.
- One drain for fuel filter located underside of wing outboard of nacelle.

_____

_____

_____

5. How is fuel system venting accomplished? (AFM)

Both the main and auxiliary fuel systems are vented through a recessed ram vent coupled to a protruding ram vent on the underside of wing tip. Recessed vent is ice resistant by design; protruding vent is heated to prevent icing.

_____

_____

_____

_____

6. Describe the operation of the fuel purge system. (AFM)

The system uses a small purge tank pressurized by the engine compressor (P3) discharge air. On engine shutdown, the purge tank pressure forces excess fuel out of the engine fuel manifold lines, through the fuel nozzles and into the engine, where the fuel is burned. Usually results in a momentary surge in N1 gas generator rpm.

_____

_____

_____

_____

7. Describe the fuel quantity indicators. (AFM)

a. Capacitance type fuel quantity indication system.

b. Fuel quantity indicators (left and right) indicate fuel (in pounds) remaining in respective fuel tanks.

c. Compensates for changes in fuel density due to temperature changes.

d. Maximum indication error of 3% full scale.

e. Fuel quantity in auxiliary tanks determined by deflecting a spring-loaded fuel quantity switch to "Aux." position.

_____

_____

_____

_____

8. How is fuel transferred from the fuel tanks to the engines? (AFM)

Engine-driven fuel pumps (high-pressure and boost) draw fuel from the collector tank. The collector tank draws fuel from its respective main tank (unless fuel is being supplied from the auxiliary tank). Auxiliary tank fuel should be used prior to using fuel in the main tanks. Accomplished by positioning auxiliary pump switches to AUTO. When no fuel is remaining in auxiliary tank, the pump automatically shuts off.

_____

_____

_____

_____

_____

9. Proper fuel management in this aircraft requires fuel from the auxiliary tanks to be used before the main tank fuel. Why? (AFM)

In the event of an auxiliary pump failure, the fuel remaining in the auxiliary tanks would not be available for flight. Backup or secondary pumps are not installed and it is not possible to gravity feed fuel from the auxiliary fuel tanks.

_____

_____

_____

10. Describe how you would cross-transfer fuel from one tank to another. (AFM)

a. Standby pump switches in OFF position.

b. Move lever lock switch (TRANSFER FLOW -OFF) from the center OFF position to the left or right, depending on direction of flow.

c. Cross-transfer valve is now open which energizes standby pump on the side from which cross-feed is desired. Green FUEL TRANSFER annunciator on caution/advisory panel will illuminate.

_____

_____

_____

11. How do the firewall shutoff valves work? (AFM)

Two firewall shutoff valves are provided, one for each engine. The valves are controlled by the FIRE PULL handles located on the upper center instrument panel. When the FIRE PULL handle is pulled, it closes the firewall shutoff valve and arms the fire extinguisher.

_____

_____

12. How does the fuel control unit work? (AFM)

The fuel control unit regulates fuel flow to the engine by metering fuel to the fuel nozzles. It compares power and condition lever position to the selected N1 (gas generator speed).

_____

_____

13. How is fuel system icing prevented? (AFM)

Via an oil-to-fuel heat exchanger, located on the engine accessory case which operates continuously.

J. Electrical System

1. Describe the electrical system. (AFM)

a. Negatively-grounded 28-volt DC system (grounded to aircraft structure).

b. 23 amp/hour NiCad battery, or optional 34 amp/hour air-cooled NiCad battery.

c. Two 28-volt, 300 amp starter/generators supply all power to DC buses and the battery (to maintain charge).

d. AC power is provided by two 115/26 VAC, 400 Hz inverters.

2. Where is the battery located? (AFM)

It is located in the right wing root between the fuselage and the right engine nacelle.

3. What volts/amps are required for starting when using an external power cart? (AFM)

External power carts should be capable of providing 28.0–28.4 volts, and a minimum of 1,000 amps momentarily and 300 amps continuously.

4. The electrical system consists of several buses. What are they? (AFM)

Two generator buses, two center buses, a battery bus, and a triple-fed bus are provided.

5. Describe how electrical power is distributed among the various buses. (AFM)

The electrical system uses the triple-fed bus arrangement, which means that most electrical system buses receive power from three power sources. Each individual bus is powered by its respective source — the battery, the left generator, and the right generator. In normal operation, all buses are automatically tied into a single loop. A hot battery bus provides power for essential equipment such as cockpit emergency lighting, threshold lighting, fire extinguishing system and the main entry door.

6. What other equipment is located on the hot battery bus? (AFM)

Left and right firewall fuel shut-off valves, external power annunciator, forward baggage door annunciator, control wheel clock, pitot heater right side, ground communication power.

7. Describe the function of the main starter/generators. (AFM)

The starter/generators act as starters for the engines up to 52% N1. Above that value, they assume the function of a generator producing 28 volts/300 amps to power the aircraft electrical buses.

8. How is generator output monitored? (AFM)

Two volt/loadmeters are provided to monitor generator output and battery charge.

9. **What are the functions of the two generator control units (GCU)?** (AFM)

   a. Voltage regulation (28.25 ±.25 volts).

   b. Line contactor control (connection of generators to electrical buses).

   c. Overvoltage protection (over 32 volts).

   d. Load sharing and paralleling (within 10%).

   e. Reverse current protection.

   f. Cross start current limiting.

   _____

   _____

   _____

10. **Three high-current-sensing devices control three bus tie relays. What is their function?** (AFM)

    Also known as HEDs (hall effect devices), these sensors actuate by opening the affected bus tie anytime they sense a current of 275 amps or higher supplied from a single source. They effectively isolate the bus requiring the high current and allow the remaining power sources to continue functioning as a system.

    _____

    _____

    _____

    _____

11. **What is the function of a line contactor relay?** (AFM)

    Line contactor relays connect power from the generators to the electrical system buses. They are also used as reverse-current devices by the generator control units. The relays prevent the generators from absorbing power from the bus when the generator voltage is less than the bus voltage.

    _____

    _____

    _____

    _____

K. Environmental

1. Describe the pressurization system on this aircraft. (AFM)

The pressurization system uses bleed air from the compressor section of each engine to pressurize the cabin. The system provides a pressure differential of 4.8 ± .1 psi. The bleed air is precooled by a heat exchanger and two valves before it enters the air cycle machine (ACM), or bypasses the ACM and is ducted to the cabin. Bleed air flow and pressure are controlled from the cockpit by the environmental bleed air shutoff valves.

_____

_____

_____

_____

2. What is the function of the pressurization controller? (AFM)

The adjustable pressurization controller commands modulation of the outflow valve. The controller has an inner and outer scale. The outer scale indicates cabin pressure altitude that the controller will maintain (set by the pilot). The inner scale indicates the maximum ambient pressure altitude the airplane can fly without causing the cabin pressure altitude to exceed the value set on the outer scale.

_____

_____

_____

_____

3. What is the function of the outflow valves? (AFM)

a. Control cabin pressure by venting excess air overboard.

b. Provide both positive and negative pressure relief.

c. Provide a means of "dumping" the cabin pressure.

_____

_____

_____

4. How is pressurization of the aircraft indicated in the cockpit? (AFM)

The actual cabin pressure altitude is indicated by a cabin altimeter, mounted on the forward panel between caution/annunciator panel and pedestal. A cabin vertical speed indicator is also provided which indicates the rate at which cabin pressure altitude is changing; it is located immediately to the left of the cabin altimeter.

5. What is the function of the cabin pressure switch? (AFM)

The cabin pressure switch allows the pilot to pressurize the aircraft, depressurize the aircraft or test the system. A three-position switch labeled DUMP, PRESS, and TEST controls the system. The DUMP position holds the outflow valves open and depressurizes the cabin. The PRESS position allows the outflow valves to be controlled by the pressurization controller. The TEST position opens the landing gear safety switch circuit, allowing the outflow valves to close. This feature allows the aircraft to be pressurized on the ground. The switch is located forward of the pressurization controller on the pedestal.

6. Describe the operation of the pressurization system. (AFM)

a. Prior to takeoff, adjust the cabin altitude selector knob so that 1,000 feet above planned cruise pressure altitude is displayed on indicator.

b. Ensure that the CAB ALT scale indicates an altitude of at least 500 feet above takeoff field pressure altitude.

Continued

c. Adjust rate controller knob as desired (setting index mark at 12 o'clock position results in 500-fpm cabin rate of climb; most comfortable).

d. Ensure that cabin pressure switch is in PRESS position.

e. The cabin pressure altitude will climb at the selected rate and once established at the pre-selected pressure altitude, the system will maintain that selected altitude.

_____

_____

_____

_____

_____

7. Describe how the pressurization system reacts to a change in altitude. (AFM)

If the altitude selected on the ACFT ALT scale is not adjusted, and the aircraft climbs, cabin-to-ambient pressure differential will reach the pressure relief setting of the outflow valves. The outflow valves will override the pressurization controller in order to maintain cabin pressure differential to 4.8 psi ± .1 psi.

_____

_____

_____

_____

8. What mechanism is used to prevent the aircraft from being pressurized on the ground? (AFM)

When the aircraft is on the ground, the landing gear safety switch on the left gear signals the outflow valves to modulate to the full open position.

_____

_____

_____

9. How does the altitude warning feature work? (AFM)

A pressure-sensing switch, located on the electrical panel of the forward aft bulkhead, will close anytime it senses a cabin pressure altitude of 12,500 feet resulting in illumination of the CABIN ALTITUDE annunciator.

10. What will happen if both bleed air valves are positioned to INST and ENVIR OFF? (AFM)

Loss of pressurization will occur. No bleed air is being supplied to the pressure vessel.

11. How can the pilot ventilate the aircraft if it is unpressurized? (AFM)

A manually-controlled valve, located in the nose ram air duct, can be opened to supply ambient air to the cabin when the airplane is not pressurized. Air enters the airplane through the ram air door solenoid valve and the manual valve when the cabin pressure control switch is set to "dump."

12. How is the aircraft heated? (AFM)

Engine bleed air is used to heat the cabin. The bleed air enters the cabin distribution ducts for heating through the air cycle machine and ejector bypass valves. When heating is required, the air cycle machine bypass valve opens and modulates output of the ACM. When maximum heating is required, the ACM bypass valve modulates to the full open position and then directs current to the ejector bypass valve, which also modulates to the full open position. The heated air is ducted to outlets in the cabin sidewalls, crew vents and defroster.

_____

_____

_____

13. How is the aircraft cooled? (AFM)

Both an air cycle system and a vapor cycle system are used to provide cabin cooling. When the air cycle system is providing maximum cooling, a signal is automatically generated by the temperature control circuitry resulting in the vapor cycle system coming online to provide further cooling. For maximum cooling, both the ejector bypass valve and the ACM bypass valves are closed and the VCM is online.

_____

_____

_____

_____

14. Describe the air cycle system. (AFM)

Air cycle machines use engine bleed air to turn a compressor that compresses air, resulting in a rise in temperature. The high-temperature air is routed through heat exchangers to remove some of the excess heat, then sent to the ACM expansion turbine. As the air passes through the turbine, it rotates the turbine and the impeller. After the compressed air performs the work of turning the turbine, it undergoes a pressure and temperature drop resulting in an air temperature significantly lower than the ambient air temperature.

_____

_____

_____

_____

_____

15. Describe the vapor cycle system. (AFM)

The vapor cycle system consists of the following:

a. *Compressor*—increases pressure of refrigerated gas when it is in vapor form. Provides force necessary to circulate gas through the system.

b. *Condensing coil and blower assembly*—removes heat from compressed high-pressure, high-temperature refrigerated gas coming from the compressor. Changes state from gas to liquid.

c. *Thermostatic expansion valve*—metering device that directs high-pressure, low-temperature refrigerated liquid to the evaporator.

d. *Evaporator*—lowers pressure of refrigerated liquid causing a change in state from liquid to gas; results in maximum cooling.

e. *Evaporator coil*—air is routed over coil where heat is removed before being returned to the cabin.

f. Low-pressure, low-temperature refrigerant is then returned to the compressor.

_____

_____

_____

_____

_____

_____

_____

16. What conditions must be met in order for the VCM to operate? (AFM)

Outside air temperature of greater than 45°F, ACM bypass valve fully closed, and the right engine is operating at 62% N1.

_____

_____

_____

L. Oxygen

1. Describe the oxygen system on this aircraft. (AFM)

a. Consists of two 76.6 foot cylinders.

b. Mounted under the floor of the nose baggage compartment.

c. Two cylinder pressure gauges on copilot right subpanel.

d. Pressure gage indicating pressure to the cabin masks right side of instrument panel.

_____

_____

_____

_____

2. What is the system pressure for the oxygen system? (AFM)

1,850 psi at 70°F.   _____

3. Describe the oxygen system for the crew. (AFM)

a. Constant-flow type (O_2 flows continuously).

b. Cylinder-mounted constant-flow regulators with reduced pressure output.

c. Two oxygen outlets and associated masks located behind the overhead light control panel.

d. Removal/insertion of a lanyard pin controls oxygen flow to the masks.

_____

_____

_____

_____

4. How are the two oxygen cylinders actuated? (AFM)

A push pull control knob labeled OXYGEN — PULL ON, simultaneously actuates the two oxygen cylinders.

5. Describe the passenger oxygen masks. (AFM)

a. Constant-flow type (O_2 flows continuously).

b. Altitude compensating.

c. Constant-flow regulator varies flow rate to masks based on altitude (mounted on left side of airplane, aft of forward pressure bulkhead).

6. How is oxygen flow to the passenger masks initiated? (AFM)

A push-pull control knob labeled CABIN OXYGEN — PULL ON, governs the flow of oxygen to the passenger oxygen outlets. The passenger must remove a lanyard valve pin from the mask to start the flow of oxygen.

7. What mechanism causes the passenger mask container door to open? (AFM)

When the push-pull control knob is pulled out, a surge valve will initially allow high pressure to reach the mask container door, causing the door to open and allowing access to the mask.

M. Pitot Static System

1. Describe the pitot-static system on this airplane. (AFM)

a. Two pitot tubes (pilot and copilot).

b. Two separate sources of normal static air; one for pilot and one for copilot.

c. Normal static air provided by static ports located on the pitot/static masts.

d. Alternate static source is provided; alternate line obtains static air from each side of the lower nose.

_____

_____

_____

_____

2. Are the static lines interconnected? (AFM)

Yes; the two static sources are connected together so that, in the event of one source becoming obstructed, both pilot and copilot instruments will still be functional from the remaining source.

_____

_____

_____

3. In the event of a failure of either pilot's normal static air source, what procedure should be followed? (AFM)

The alternate static source should be selected by lifting a spring-clip retainer off the pilot or copilot's static air source valve switch, and then moving that switch to the ALTERNATE position.
Note: When using an alternate static air source, the altimeter, airspeed and vertical speed instrument indications will be affected.

_____

_____

_____

_____

N. Engine Bleed Air Pneumatic System

1. What are some of the aircraft systems that utilize engine bleed air? (AFM)

Cabin pressurization, heating and cooling, brake deice, deice boots, hydraulic system, vacuum system.

2. Bleed air is obtained from which engine stage? (AFM)

P3

3. What is the approximate temperature of bleed air? (AFM)

800°F. Precooled to 450°F before use by the environmental system (pressurization/air conditioning).

4. Describe the bleed air warning system. (AFM)

EVA tubing (plastic) pressurized to 18 psi is co-located with the bleed air ducting running from the engines to the cabin. Any excessive heat caused by a bleed air duct rupture would cause the EVA tubing to melt resulting in an immediate drop in pressure. The drop in pressure causes a switch in the line to close illuminating the L or R BL AIR FAIL annunciator in the warning annunciator panel.

5. What is the function of the bleed air valve switches? (AFM)

In the event of a bleed-air line failure, bleed air for that particular line may be shut off by positioning the BLEED AIR VALVE switch on the FO's left subpanel in the INSTR and ENVIR OFF position.

6. **What is normal pneumatic system pressure regulated at?** (AFM)

   18 psi

7. **How is pneumatic pressure used to create vacuum for the vacuum system?** (AFM)

   Vacuum is created by directing pneumatic air through a bleed air ejector.

8. **What aircraft systems use vacuum for operation?** (AFM)

   a. Aircraft flight instruments (directional gyro and attitude indicator).

   b. Surface deice system (deflates deice boots).

   c. Pressurization system (outflow valves, pressurization controller).

9. **What is the vacuum system pressure regulated at?** (AFM)

   4.3" to 5.9" Hg

O. Ice Protection

1. **What are the two basic types of ice protection equipment?** (AFM)

   Anti-ice and deice.

2. **What are some of the anti-ice systems on this airplane?** (AFM)

   Engine air inlet lip heat, inertial separators, pitot heat, static port heat, windshield heat, stall warning vane heat, fuel vent heat, oil-to-fuel heat exchanger.

3. What are some of the deice systems on this airplane? (AFM)

Brake deice, surface deice (boots), propeller deice.

4. What effect does placing the windshield anti-ice switch in the NORM and HI positions have? (AFM)

NORM — A major portion of the windshield is supplied with heat.

HI — A higher level of heat is supplied to a smaller area of the windshield.

5. Describe the propeller electric deice system. (AFM)

a. Electrically-heated deice boots

b. Slip rings and brush block assemblies

c. Timer for automatic operation

d. Dual-scale ammeter

e. Two prop deice control circuit breakers

f. Circuit breakers and current limiters for protection of prop deice boot wiring

g. Two switches for auto or manual control of system

6. Describe the operational sequence of the propeller deice system when the switch is in the AUTO position. (AFM)

When the switch placarded PROP-AUTO is selected to AUTO, the propeller automatic timer supplies power to the heating elements of one propeller for 90 seconds. Then it automatically switches over to supply power to the other propeller for 90 seconds. Each cycle takes approximately 3 minutes.

_____

_____

_____

7. Describe the operational sequence of the propeller deice system when the switch is held in the MANUAL position. (AFM)

When the switch placarded PROP-MANUAL is held in the MANUAL position, the heating elements on both of the propellers are supplied power. The switch should be held in the MANUAL position for approximately 90 seconds.

_____

_____

_____

_____

8. How is normal operation of the propeller deice system be verified in the cockpit? (AFM)

With the propeller deice switch in the ON position, normal operation of the propeller deice system can be accomplished by monitoring normal current flow to each propeller blade of 26 to 32 amps on a dual-scale ammeter located on the overhead panel.

_____

_____

_____

_____

9. What type of ice protection is provided for the engines? (AFM)

a. *Engine air inlet*—engine exhaust is used for heating air inlet lips. The hot exhaust is collected by a scoop and ducted downward to connect with inlet lip.

b. *Engine anti-ice* — inertial separation system is provided in each engine air duct; prevents moisture from entering the engine inlet plenum during icing conditions.

_____

_____

10. What aerodynamic surfaces are protected by the surface deice system? (AFM)

The leading edges of the wings, stabilons, and horizontal stabilizers.

_____

11. Describe the operation of the surface deice system. (AFM)

Pressure-regulated engine bleed air supplies the necessary pressure to inflate the boots. The vacuum needed to hold the boots in the deflated position is created by bleed air directed through a venturi ejector. A distributor valve controls the inflation and deflation cycles.

_____

_____

_____

_____

12. Describe the sequence of deice boot inflation when the surface deice switch is in the SINGLE position. (AFM)

a. Distributor valve opens to send bleed air to outboard wing boots for 6 seconds.

b. Electronic timer switches distributor to deflate outboard boots.

c. Electronic timer opens distributor to inflate inboard wing boots, horizontal stabilizer and stabilon boots for 6 seconds then deflates. Cycle is now complete.

_____

_____

_____

_____

13. Describe the sequence of deice boot inflation when the surface deice switch is held in the MANUAL position. (AFM)

All the boots will inflate simultaneously and remain that way until the switch is returned to the OFF position.

_____

_____

14. When must the auto ignition system be armed? (AFM)

During takeoff, landing, turbulence, and anytime the aircraft is being operated in icing conditions or heavy precipitation. Also used for takeoffs from contaminated runways. Prevents engine loss due to combustion failure (engine flame out).

_____

_____

_____

_____

BE-1900
Limitations   Appendix B

The following questions are in reference to the Beechcraft 1900-C limitations.

These questions are representative of what you are required to know about your aircraft limitations. Review your aircraft's AFM for answers specific to the airplane your checkride will take place in.

The blank lines can be used to document the information for aircraft you will be flying or testing in other than the BE-1900.

A. Airspeed Limitations

1. What is V_A? (AFM)

V_A (16,600) 188 KIAS _____

2. What is V_{FE} at the takeoff position (10% flap deflection)? (AFM)

198 KIAS _____

3. What is V_{FE} at the approach position (40% flap deflection)? (AFM)

168 KIAS _____

4. What is V_{FE} at the down position (100% flap deflection)? (AFM)

153 KIAS _____

5. What is V_{LO}? (AFM)

Extension—180 KIAS _____

Retraction—180 KIAS _____

6. What is V_{LE}? (AFM)

180 KIAS _____

7. What is V_{MO}/M_{MO}? (AFM)

V_{MO}—247 KIAS _____

M_{MO}—.48 Mach _____

8. What is V_{MCA}? (AFM)

Flaps up.. 96 KIAS

Takeoff flaps..................................... 91 KIAS

Approach flaps................................. 89 KIAS

9. What is the maximum demonstrated crosswind component? (AFM)

22 knots _____

10. What is the two-engine best angle-of-climb (V_X) speed? (AFM)

122 knots _____

11. What is the two-engine best rate-of-climb (V_Y) speed? (AFM)

138 knots (decrease 2 knots per 5,000 feet) _____

12. What airspeed should be used for cruise climb airspeed? (AFM)

Sea level to 10,000 feet.................... 160 knots _____

10,000 to 15,000 feet .... 150 knots _____

15,000 to 20,000 feet .... 140 knots _____

20,000 to 25,000 feet .... 130 knots _____

13. What is the recommended turbulent air penetration airspeed? (AFM)

170 knots _____

14. What is the minimum speed for operations in icing conditions? (AFM)

160 KIAS _____

15. What is the minimum airspeed to air-start the engine without using starter assist? (AFM)

140 KIAS _____

16. What is the maximum windshield anti-icing speed? (AFM)

223 KIAS _____

B. Emergency Airspeeds (at 16,600 pounds)

1. What is the one-engine-inoperative best angle-of-climb (V_{XSE}) airspeed? (AFM)

120 knots _____

2. What is the one-engine-inoperative best rate-of-climb (V_{YSE}) airspeed? (AFM)

125 knots _____

3. What is the one-engine-inoperative best enroute climb (V_{ENR}) airspeed? (AFM)

125 knots _____

4. What are the minimum control airspeeds (V_{MCA}) airspeeds? (AFM)

Flaps up.. 96 knots _____

Flaps takeoff .... 91 knots _____

Flaps approach............................... 89 knots _____

5. **What airspeed should be used in an emergency descent?** (AFM)

180 knots _____

6. **What airspeed should be used for a maximum-range glide?** (AFM)

125 knots _____

C. Powerplant Limitations

1. **What is the maximum ITT for start?** (AFM)

1,000°C _____

2. **What is the maximum allowable ITT for takeoff?** (AFM)

820°C limited to 5 minutes _____

3. **What is the maximum continuous torque?** (AFM)

3,400 foot-pounds _____

4. **What is the maximum allowable transient torque?** (AFM)

5,000 foot-pounds for 20 seconds _____

5. **In the event that a starter-assisted air-start must be performed, engine ITT must be reduced to what value?** (AFM)

700°C or below _____

6. **What is the maximum propeller overspeed limit?** (AFM)

1,870 for 20 seconds _____

7. **What is the maximum rpm for takeoff?** (AFM)

1,700 rpm _____

8. What is the maximum propeller rpm? (AFM)

1,870 rpm

9. What is maximum reverse propeller rpm? (AFM)

1,650 rpm

10. When should an aborted start be performed? (AFM)

If no rise in ITT occurs within 10 seconds after introducing fuel.

11. What is the minimum oil pressure at flight idle? (AFM)

60 psi

12. What are the minimum and maximum N1 values? (AFM)

58% and 104%

13. What are the compressor (gas generator) shaft rotational speed (N1) limits? (AFM)

At takeoff/maximum continuous/cruise climb/maximum cruise power, 104.0% N1 (39,000 rpm).

14. What is the oil quantity for this engine? (AFM)

System capacity is 15.6 quarts or 3.9 gallons. Oil quantity range is MAX to 4 QUARTS LOW on dipstick.

15. What is the maximum outside operating air temperature? (AFM)

ISA plus 37°C

16. What are oil temperature limitations? (AFM)

-40°C to +99°C; 110°C for up to 10 minutes.

17. The autofeather mechanism is disabled at what engine setting? (AFM)

550 foot-pounds

18. While in cruise flight, what oil pressure would require engine shut down? (AFM)

Below 60 psi

19. What are the minimum and maximum oil temperature limits? (AFM)

-40°C to +99°C; a maximum temperature of +110°C for no more than 10 minutes.

20. What is the minimum recommended oil temperature for fuel heater operation at takeoff power? (AFM)

+55°C

21. While in cruise flight, what oil pressure would require engine shut down? (AFM)

Below 60 psi

D. Electrical System

1. What is the maximum differential between generator loadmeters? (AFM)

10%

2. What is the minimum voltage for battery start? (AFM)

23 VDC

3. What is the maximum generator load during ground operations? (AFM)

100% with air conditioning off

4. At what N1 value will the starter/generators "start" function stop and "generator" function begin? (AFM)

At or above 52% N1 _____

5. What are the starter operating limitations? (AFM)

30 seconds ON _____

3 minutes OFF _____

30 seconds ON _____

30 minutes OFF _____

6. What are the generator limitations? (AFM)

0 to 50% generator load—air conditioning ON....................65% N1
      air conditioning OFF.......................................58% N1

_____

50 to 75% generator load—air conditioning ON.................70% N1
      air conditioning OFF.......................................60% N1

_____

75 to 100% generator load—air conditioning ON...............72% N1
      air conditioning OFF.......................................72% N1

_____

7. What is the required power output of an external power cart used for engine starting? (AFM)

28.0 – 28.4 volts and 1,000 amps momentarily and 300 amps continuously. _____

8. What is the required power output of an external power cart used for engine starting? (AFM)

28.0 – 28.4 volts and 1,000 amps momentarily and 300 amps continuously. _____

9. Where is the external power supply receptacle located? (AFM)

Under the aft portion of the left nacelle. _____

E. Fuel System

1. What is the usable capacity of the main tanks at 6.64 density? (AFM)

241.3 gallons/1,626.5 pounds _____

2. What is the usable capacity of the auxiliary fuel tanks? (AFM)

92.3 galllons/622 pounds _____

3. What is the maximum useable fuel quantity? (AFM)

667.2 gallons/4,497 pounds _____

4. What is the maximum usable fuel quantity in each wing tank? (AFM)

333.6 gallons/2,248.5 pounds _____

5. What minimum fuel is required for takeoff? (AFM)

363 lbs in each wing system; do not take off if fuel quantity gauges are in the yellow arc. _____

6. What are the approved engine fuels available for use in this engine? (AFM)

Commercial—Jet A, Jet A-1, Jet B _____

Military—JP-4, JP-5, JP-8 _____

7. Is it possible to use AVGAS in this engine, in the event approved fuels are unavailable? (AFM)

Yes; operation is limited to no more than 150 hours between engine overhauls. Flight altitude is limited to below 15,000 feet.

_____

_____

8. **What is the minimum fuel pressure?** (AFM)

100 psi   _____

9. **How many fuel drains are located on each wing?** (AFM)

6   _____

10. **What is the engine-driven fuel pump pressure?** (AFM)

850 psi   _____

11. **What is the output pressure of the standby pump?** (AFM)

30 – 45 psi   _____

12. **What is the engine-driven boost pump pressure?** (AFM)

45 psi   _____

13. **What is the minimum fuel temperature for Jet A?** (AFM)

-40°C   _____

14. **What is the maximum demonstrated imbalance between left and right fuel tanks?** (AFM)

200 pounds   _____

F. Weight and CG Limitations

1. **What is the maximum ramp weight?** (AFM)

16,710 pounds   _____

2. **What is the maximum takeoff weight?** (AFM)

16,600 pounds   _____

3. **What is the maximum landing weight?** (AFM)

16,100 pounds   _____

4. What is maximum zero fuel weight? (AFM)

14,000 pounds

5. What is the maximum weight in the baggage compartments? (AFM)

Nose—150 pounds

Forward cabin compartment—250 pound

Hangar, Forward Cabin Compartment—100 pounds

Aft baggage compartment (fwd section)—880 pounds

Aft baggage compartment (aft section)—630 pounds

6. What are the load factor maneuvering limitations? (AFM)

Takeoff flaps and flaps up—3.00 positive Gs; 1.20 negative Gs

Flaps approach and landing—2.00 positive Gs; 0.00 negative Gs

7. What is the maximum cabin floor loading? (AFM)

100 lbs/sq. ft.

8. What are the aft and forward CG limits in inches aft of datum? (AFM)

Aft limit: 299.9 inches aft of datum for all weights.

Forward limit: 282.2 inches aft of datum at 16,600 pounds to 274.5 inches aft of datum at 11,600 pounds.

9. Where is the reference datum located? (AFM)

83.5 inches forward of the center of the front jack point.

G. Other Limitations

1. What category is the BE-1900 certified under? (AFM)

Normal _____

2. Where are the emergency exits located? (AFM)

The main cabin door and 3 overwing exits are provided.

_____

3. What are the outside air temperature limitations? (AFM)

ISA plus 37°C for operations from sea level to 25,000 feet pressure altitude.

_____

4. What is the minimum flight crew for the BE-1900? (AFM)

One pilot _____

5. What is the maximum passenger occupancy limitation? (AFM)

Nineteen _____

6. What are the normal and maximum pressure differentials? (AFM)

Normal— 4.8 psid _____

Maximum—4.9 psid _____

7. What is the maximum cabin altitude? (AFM)

12,500 feet _____

8. At what value is normal environmental system pressure maintained? (AFM)

38 psi _____

9. **At what rate is temperature-controlled air delivered to the pressure vessel?** (AFM)

    8–16 ppm　　　　　　＿＿＿＿＿＿＿＿＿＿＿＿＿＿＿

10. **What is maximum sea level cabin altitude?** (AFM)

    10,500 feet　　　　　＿＿＿＿＿＿＿＿＿＿＿＿＿＿＿

11. **What is the design service ceiling?** (AFM)

    25,000 feet　　　　　＿＿＿＿＿＿＿＿＿＿＿＿＿＿＿

12. **What is the minimum N1 necessary to maintain adequate airflow in flight?** (AFM)

    75%　　　　　　　　＿＿＿＿＿＿＿＿＿＿＿＿＿＿＿

13. **What are the tire pressures for the main gear and nose-gear tires?** (AFM)

    Main gear—95 psi　　＿＿＿＿＿＿＿＿＿＿＿＿＿＿＿

    Nose gear—60 psi　　＿＿＿＿＿＿＿＿＿＿＿＿＿＿＿

14. **What is the maximum tailwind component?** (AFM)

    10 knots　　　　　　＿＿＿＿＿＿＿＿＿＿＿＿＿＿＿

15. **What is the maximum demonstrated crosswind component?** (AFM)

    25 knots　　　　　　＿＿＿＿＿＿＿＿＿＿＿＿＿＿＿

16. **What is the maximum landing gear cycle limit?** (AFM)

    The gear may be cycled three times allowing 2 minutes between cycles. Each additional landing gear cycle requires a 5-minute interval between cycles.

Notes